"NJOY the BOOK
and KEEP the FAITH "

THE GOP'S LOST DECADE

AN INSIDE VIEW OF
WHY WASHINGTON DOESN'T WORK
BY JIM RENACCI

The 94 new members elected to the House of Representatives in 2010.
Eighty-five of the freshmen were Republicans.

ISBN 978-1-7321855-1-7

Library of Congress Control Number: 2019908282
Cover and book design: 30 Point

BETHESDA, MARYLAND

CONTENTS

INTRODUCTION

WHY CONGRESS DOESN'T WORK

The first thing I learned about Washington is that nothing starts on time. As a businessman, I have always prided myself on being punctual when I attend meetings. My first boss taught me, if you can't be on time, be early. That's not the case in Washington. Usually, I arrived early for everything, as my staff would tell you. But outside of my own office in Washington, I was frequently waiting in empty rooms for fifteen or twenty minutes — sometimes longer — before anyone else showed up.

It may seem like a small thing, but it isn't. Nothing in Washington starts on time because no one puts a priority on meetings. Staff dictates schedules, and so many meetings get stacked back-to-back that most days quickly devolve into a race through the calendar. There are no priorities. You just run through the events of the day. In many cases, every issue, regardless of its significance, receives the same sense of urgency. As a result, even meetings that could be important are treated as just another chore. Members of Congress show up when they can, often without allowing enough time to resolve or discuss an issue. They rely on their staffs to sort things out because of the time constraints, and they often wind up ignoring their constituents. Meetings frequently end without accomplishing anything, which means another meeting has to be scheduled. That next one, too, will start late, and the cycle continues. Members' perpetual tardiness is a living testament to their inefficiency and ineffectiveness.

A decade ago, I decided to go to Washington because I wanted to change the way that our government operated. Almost as soon as I got there, I began to see why the system was so broken. During the next eight years, I became increasingly frustrated by the pervasive dysfunction.

For more than thirty years, I've been building a career running different businesses that all had one thing in common: They faced problems that needed fixing. I turned around everything from nursing homes to car dealerships, so I thought I knew how to tackle the big problems Washington faced. Rather than complain about the government, I ran for office because I believed the skills I had developed over the course of my business career could help get our government back on track and get it working for the people once again. There were also others who came into Congress with me who felt the same way. Ten years ago, we were all going to change Washington.

But almost from the moment I arrived, I began running into entrenched attitudes and processes. Washington wasn't working because no one had an incentive to make it work. Creating good policy, passing meaningful legislation, compromising with others in support of our democratic ideals — these simply weren't priorities for most people working inside the Beltway.

Sometimes, this intransigence related to big issues, such as the process (or lack thereof) for creating the federal budget. Sometimes, the examples were small, perhaps almost insignificant. But they all spoke to a stubborn refusal to change.

The second thing I noticed about Washington was a profound lack of financial understanding — or even a desire for understanding. There's little appreciation for the cost of legislation. The Congressional Budget Office, which is supposed to be nonpartisan, and the Office of Management and Budget many times play games with financial projections, and lawmakers themselves often fail to see — or simply ignore — the financial consequences of their decisions. Few people seem to know or care how much anything costs or whether there is any return on an investment. To make matters worse, the government doesn't operate by the same financial rules that most businesses and households do, and, as a result, it's easy for lawmakers to disregard the costs of their actions. Their disregard is obscured by the ease with which the federal government borrows money it doesn't have.

The third problem, which will be less surprising to most voters, is that politics always gets in the way of every decision made. Political gain takes precedence over legislative achievement. Although I could see this from the outside — in fact, it had a lot to do with my decision to run for Congress in the first place — what I found surprising was the extent to which politics overrode everything we tried to do. Time and again, a Democrat would propose a bill that all the other Democrats voted for and all the Republicans voted against. Or vice versa. It didn't matter if it was a good bill or a bad one. It's about who has the power and how that power can be maintained.

The focus is never on the bill itself or what was best for the country. Politics today is a zero-sum game in which the majority wants to push its agenda, and the minority wants to impede that agenda. When I look back at all the bills that Congress passed during my eight years there, few, if any, were truly developed by the traditional process for passing legislation, and most were not bipartisan. Even representatives who advocated for bipartisanship would wind up voting with party leadership more often than not because they needed support from their party's leaders to get reelected.

Newer lawmakers, like cattle going to the feed trough, voted the way their leadership told them to, because that was the only way they could ever hope to earn their support, pass something legislatively or even get into leadership themselves. Everyone is chasing political power, which really translates into the ability to stay. Many party leaders come from districts with few political challengers, and this "safety" back home allows them to focus on building their power base in Washington. The result is both parties develop leadership that's more concerned with staying in Washington and maintaining the power of their office than working for the good of the country.

The bottom line is simple. If you don't start on time, don't know where you stand financially, and you let political agendas override everything you do, you will never accomplish anything. And that is the state of our government.

When I was first elected, I thought that, as most of us learned in high school civics classes, lawmakers went to Washington to represent the people. My personal experience showed me that government is broken, and that it has lost sight of the consequences of its actions. My hopes to change the system were ground down by the inertia of the status quo. Congress is a den of dysfunction. It is a body that lacks the fortitude to do what's right. And as that dysfunction has grown, we have managed to make the situation far worse because we are afraid to try to make it better.

I came into Congress in 2011, riding the wave of the Tea Party. I was not a Tea Party member myself, but I respected their desire to change government. I shared it up to a point, but I didn't agree with all of their views on what that change should look like.

We believed we were going to change the world, or at least, change the way government worked. Ninety-four of us charged in, full of enthusiasm. Ten years later, we limped out with just forty-two of us left. Nothing had changed. We didn't accomplish any of the things we set out to do. Most of us left in frustration. (In fairness, a few ran for higher office or were appointed to the Trump administration). Ten years after we started down the path to get elected and change our government, things have only gotten worse.

This isn't surprising. I found that the most qualified people in Congress usually got out in a couple of terms. Like me, they grew frustrated that they couldn't get anything done and decided to go do something else. Others, of course, see Congress as a career, and they are happy to change the rules or bend them to ensure they continue to stay.

In my experience, politicians come into office either willing to fight for their convictions or willing to follow the party line. Those that follow the party line just become part of the problem. Those that fight eventually get frustrated and leave, or they give up and become part of the problem.

In short, the way Congress functions today is not how I believed our government was supposed to work. I thought that our government was based on the concept that people should work hard in the real world, get real life experience and then go to Washington to give back using those experiences to guide them, to serve the best interests of the country. Too often today, people are running for office in a quest for glamour and power, rather than from a sense of service.

Many people, of course, complain about government gridlock and the divisiveness of politics. The fact that our government isn't working is obvious to many Americans. You may be frustrated with Washington, and if you're a Republican, you may be frustrated with what happened — or didn't happen — in Congress during the past decade. You should be. For all the control that the GOP had, we accomplished nothing that we set out to do. Ten years after we were going to change the world, we still don't have a balanced budget. Our deficits have grown, spending continues to rise, executive power has expanded, and the government's gotten bigger, not smaller. Nor did we succeed on policy — no border wall, no immigration reform, no repeal of Obamacare, no progress on social issues such as abortion or gay marriage. It may be one of the greatest missed opportunities in American history — a lost decade that should have been a time of great triumph. If we don't understand what happened, nothing will ever change.

I tried fixing the system from the inside, and I didn't succeed. No one can. Now, I hope you'll join me in trying to fix it from the outside.

I hope that in reading this book, you will come to understand why Washington is broken and why good people don't want to go to work there anymore. Quite simply, it's broken because we allow it to be broken. The system has fundamental problems that need changing. Most of all, though, I hope this book will help you understand why and how we need to do that.

THE LETTER

In May 2009, a letter arrived in a stack of daily mail at my Chevrolet dealership in Wadsworth, Ohio, a town of about 20,000 near Akron that I have called home for more than thirty-five years. I'd owned the dealership for about five years. I had already had a successful business career by then, and I hadn't intended to get into the car business. But General Motors came to me and asked me to take over what had been a troubled dealership and turn it around after seeing my success in reviving several Harley-Davidson franchises in Ohio.

I ripped open the envelope by reflex and scanned it casually. It quickly caught my attention. The letterhead was from General Motors' corporate headquarters in Detroit. I had to read it twice for the full impact of the message to sink in. "You will no longer be a part of the General Motors family ..." GM would not renew my franchise to operate and I had fifteen months to wind down the business. I felt as if I'd been kicked in the stomach. What was going on? I had a good working relationship with GM. After all, the company had encouraged me to buy the dealership, and I had turned it around. Sales were up. We were both happy with how things were going.

I quickly realized that the letter probably had little to do with GM itself. The automaker and its longtime rival Chrysler were in serious financial trouble, ostensibly as a result of the financial crisis and bad management. GMAC, the carmaker's financing arm, had gotten into mortgages years earlier, which compounded problems of rising costs that had been festering within GM for years. The company wasn't bankrupt yet, but it soon would be.

That posed a problem for Barack Obama, who had been president only for a few months. GM employed tens of thousands of union workers, and union support was vitally important to the Democratic Party. Officially, GM was closing lower-volume dealerships — principally those in smaller markets — to strengthen the remaining network. But GM's problems really weren't with its dealer network. It was with internal costs, largely because of its union contracts. About $2,000 of the sticker price for every vehicle went just to cover union health benefits and retirement expenses. It was those so-called legacy costs added to the price of the vehicle. The company's cost structure couldn't compete with more nimble foreign competitors, many of which had opened nonunion U.S. manufacturing plants.

Four months before the letter arrived, Obama had appointed Steven Rattner, a former Wall Street financier, to head the White House's auto industry task force. The U.S. Treasury had been lending GM money for months to help it stave off pervasive losses. In all, the government would pump some $80 billion into the carmaker, which gave Rattner tremendous influence. When the company finally did file for bankruptcy, the government basically dictated its reorganization plan.

It was Rattner who pushed the dealership closing plan, and he handed both GM and Chrysler a list of "suggestions" for which dealerships to close. Supposedly, the companies had the final say, but I would later become suspicious that the administration had targeted dealers, such as me, who were Republican donors. Regardless of the rationale, it seemed that the government had decided my dealership needed to close as part of its GM bailout.

I had spent my whole life building businesses. I had 53 employees at that dealership, and they were going to be put out of work. The government was going to take it all away from me. It seemed, well, un-American.

After all, my dealership was caught up in a much bigger scheme in which the U.S. government was basically stepping into a private company and giving it money to avoid the full consequences of its business decisions. Now, if I had made business decisions that ultimately didn't work out, and my business was on the verge of failure, and my creditors were circling, I would have to file for bankruptcy. And then I'd have to work out a plan for repaying my creditors as best I could, all under the watchful eye of a federal judge.

But GM didn't have to do that. The government, saying the already-struggling economy couldn't afford the loss of so many jobs, decided that rather than closing plants or selling divisions to repay creditors, it would cut its distribution network. If you look at other major bankruptcies — LTV Steel in Cleveland, for example — pensions are one of the first liabilities wiped out. But in GM's bankruptcy, even though its pensions were underfunded, it kept the retirement plans intact for the United Auto Workers. Instead, the government decreed that it would shed the pensions only for its Delphi parts division employees, who were nonunion. In fact, the GM "bankruptcy" was really a government takeover because the feds' assumption of debt made them the biggest creditor, much as if they had become an owner in the company. No other company had ever gone bankrupt like this.

The closing of my dealership, and the 1,100 others by GM, was just another government-mandated dodge, an attempt to cut liabilities that really weren't at the core of GM's problems. And think of the jobs that went with that. In Ohio alone, GM shuttered 152 dealerships, costing the state about six thousand jobs. They weren't autoworker jobs, but that's still a big hit to the statewide workforce. Even worse, the loss of those jobs and the cost of closing those dealerships did nothing to fix GM's legacy cost issues or their production inefficiencies that would come back to haunt the company ten years later in places like Lordstown, Ohio.

After the initial shock wore off, the anger began to set in. I started calling everyone I could at GM, and no one was calling me back. Finally, I searched through my phone log and decided to call the regional vice president who not only had convinced me to buy the dealership but also had assured me I was one of the dealers who wouldn't be affected by the bankruptcy. I dialed using the "*67" prefix, which would mask my incoming number on his phone. The number was for his cellphone, and it was after dinner. I figured he might pick up if he didn't recognize the number. He did.

"This is Jim Renacci," I said, "and I ..."

"I can't talk to you," he said. "I'm not allowed to talk to you."

"You know," I said, "I thought I was going to be a part of the General Motors family forever."

"Jim," he said slowly, "you got screwed."

Then, he hung up.

👾 👾 👾

After I got elected, some people learned that I was one of the ten wealthiest members of Congress. You would never have known that from where I lived, what I drove or my work ethic. It may have been true, but context matters. If you look at where I started, I could just as easily have ended up one of the ten poorest.

I was born in western Pennsylvania in 1958 and grew up about twenty miles south of Pittsburgh, near the Monongahela River. My house was almost in Donora, but our mailing address was Monongahela. It was a blue-collar town, and most of the men grew up to work either in the coal mines or the steel mills around Pittsburgh. My father was an exception. He worked as a car inspector for the Donora Southern Railroad, a three-mile-long short line owned by U.S. Steel that served the mills and other industries along the river. My mother was a nurse who worked the 11 p.m. to 7 a.m. shift at Monongahela Valley Hospital. She would come home from a shift an hour after my dad had left for work. Our school bus came at 6:30 a.m., so my older sisters and I had to get ourselves up, make our own breakfast and get ourselves off to school every day. That taught me independence at an early age.

My parents had grown up in the area. Especially in those days, in small towns in Pennsylvania, people didn't leave. It was quite common for most folks to live their entire lives in or near the towns they were born in. My paternal grandparents, who lived five doors down from us, came to Pennsylvania from Ponticino, Italy, in about 1920. My grandfather worked in the coal mines — that was the job that drew them to the area — but he and my grandmother also opened a little sandwich shop in the front of their house, selling meats and small food items. They believed that anything was possible in America, and they instilled that insight in me as a child. My grandfather used to tell me to work hard, do the right thing and save money. I would ask how much I should save, and he would say, "50 percent of everything you make." I'd ask what to do with the other 50 percent, and he'd say, "Save 50 percent of that, too." He didn't believe in debt, but that wasn't enough to save him as the Depression set in. Nobody could pay, and he couldn't afford to extend credit because he didn't have any money either. Eventually, he had to close the shop.

My father saw their struggles growing up, and it affected his own views. He shared their belief in doing the right thing and working hard, but he developed an even greater dislike for debt than his father. Years later, when I told my father I was taking out a loan to buy my first nursing home, he told me I was making the biggest mistake of my life. "Debt will destroy you," he said. I didn't share my parents' and grandparents' aversion to debt, although I recognized the dangers. Many years later, I would wish my fellow members of Congress could have heard my father's and grandfather's message. But I also recognized that times had changed, and I was willing to take risks to seize opportunity. What my dad and grandfather didn't realize was that controlled debt, loans that had a purpose and that could be repaid with cash flow, made sense to use in building a business. As long as the debt didn't exceed a company's asset value, and you had the cash flow to make the payments, it was OK. At the peak of my business career, I was probably carrying about $80 million in debt. My grandfather would have been shocked, even though I was still following his advice and saving half of everything I earned. The important thing was that his values of hard work and doing the right thing stuck with me.

I know it's a cliché for politicians to talk about their humble beginnings, but in my case, it's the truth. We didn't live in a mansion or have fancy clothes. My mother hates it when I say we were poor, but we were. She is quick to point out that we always had what we needed, and she's right, but it was a struggle. We had one car growing up. I remember a 1968 Ford Mustang when I was about ten years old. Somehow, all five of us managed to squeeze into it.

It wasn't an easy living, but we got by. We lived in a four-room house — two bedrooms, a kitchen, a living room and an unfinished basement. My parents had one of the bedrooms and my sisters and I shared the other, which was divided by a partition my dad put down the middle. My dad sold that house in the 1990s for $6,000. Like I said, it wasn't a mansion, but it was all we needed.

Because money was tight and there really was no one to watch us if my parents were working, they got us out of the house as early as possible. So, I started first grade at age five.

When I was eight years old, my father lost his job. He hadn't been as entrepreneurial as his father. He believed you get a good job with a good company and work hard at it to provide for your family. He lost his job thinking that way. That was a shock, because I saw my friends' fathers leaving for work in the mill every day and coming home. I saw them having regular jobs, and my dad struggled for a long time. His belief in hard work was unwavering, though, and he found odd jobs from then on to keep money coming in. I remember him leaving the house every day, looking for work, which sometimes meant digging ditches or whatever else he could find.

One afternoon, I came home from school and saw several of our neighbors, all mill workers, sitting on the porch. I knew all my neighbors as uncles, even though we weren't related. It was that kind of neighborhood. So, the other men on our street were "Uncle Bob" or "Uncle Muggs," rather than "mister." I asked Uncle Muggs why he and the others on the porch were home in the middle of the afternoon. He said they were on vacation. Sixteen-week vacations were part of the union-negotiated contract at the mill. My dad didn't have any vacation. Every day, he was out looking for a job that would bring home enough to put food on the table that night.

I wore hand-me-down clothes from our neighbors' kids when my parents couldn't afford to buy me new ones. The only tennis shoes I had were what we called fish heads — cheap canvas sneakers that cost about $1 at the time. Many of my friends had Converses, but I wouldn't get my first pair of All Stars until I made the basketball team in eighth grade and was issued a pair.

Eventually, my dad's belief in hard work paid off. He found a job selling appliances at Montgomery Ward's, and then a friend helped him get a job selling building supplies in Pittsburgh. He ended up as a general manager. He made it work, and he never gave up, and watching him I learned valuable lessons about perseverance, determination, and believing in yourself.

That entire part of western Pennsylvania was all Democratic back then, and I remember my grandparents had a picture of Franklin Delano Roosevelt on their walls. I like to say that there wasn't a Republican within 100 miles of where I grew up, and while it may be an exaggeration, I'm not off by much.

Although my parents didn't have a lot of money, they did have principles. They taught my sisters and me that if we wanted something, we would have to work for it, just like they did. My dad believed that sports were important, and he was proud when I made the basketball team or baseball team, but he also wanted to make sure I kept things in perspective. One day, as I left the house for basketball practice, my dad stopped me and held out a hammer. "This will get you a lot further in life than that basketball," he said. A neighbor down the street had a body shop, and my father encouraged me to go there on Saturdays and learn how to do body work. That way, he said, I'd always know how to do something if I needed work or money someday. Another neighbor had a roofing business, and my dad said, "Look, I don't have any money for you, but John next door will pay you if you help him put roofs on. Oh, and by the way, you'll have another trade that you'll know." So, in the summers I did roof repair and body work to make money, and I set half of it aside.

My sisters didn't go to college because my parents couldn't afford to send them, but my mother knew I'd been saving my money, and she begged me to go. I really didn't want to go. The steel mills paid well at that time, and some of my older friends who had jobs there were driving nice cars, had bought boats or even owned a small house. But my mom begged me to at least give college a try, and, eventually, I relented. I had decided I wanted to be a police officer, because I thought that it would be a good job and it would keep me out of the mills and the mines. My mother didn't like the idea, but I wasn't keen on going to college because I knew I would have to work to help pay for it. Eventually, we compromised. I would go to college like my mom wanted, and when I got out, I could become a cop if I still wanted to. I applied to Penn State, West Virginia and Indiana University of Pennsylvania.

I got accepted at all three, and I had several friends going to West Virginia, so I thought I'd go there. My father had other ideas. By then, he was a salesman for the building supply company, and he had a big client in Indiana, Pennsylvania. He told me I was going to IUP because he could get me there. My dad was a simple guy, and he was proud. He couldn't take off work to drop me off at college, so by going to IUP he could drop me off at my dorm on his way to a sales call. He used the excuse that since one of the other boys in the neighborhood was going there, it was good enough for me, too. I understood. Money was tight, and IUP was easier to get to. My mother came along to drop me off at the start of my freshman year. It was a proud moment for them. I was the first one in my family to go to college.

Once I got to school, I learned something about myself. Numbers came easily to me, and so did statistics. I hadn't had much exposure to statistics in high school, but in college, I found the subject interesting. So, I decided to pursue a degree in business administration, and I soon found that accounting also came easy to me as well. More important, I enjoyed it. Putting myself through school was a struggle. It gave me a taste of what my parents must have endured raising three children on a nurse's salary and the intermittent income my dad could scrape together. I drove a truck delivering building supplies from a distributor in downtown Pittsburgh to customers all over western Pennsylvania. I did maintenance work at a Chevrolet dealership, worked on a road crew for a couple of summers, and had a job at a school lunch packaging plant where I loaded trucks in the evening. Nothing was worse than going home after a long night of loading the trucks with milk spilled all over you. My clothes were sweaty and reeked horribly from the milk, and it made the whole house smell like an abandoned dairy. But I was working, making money and getting my education.

I graduated in 1980, earned my CPA certification, and went to work for an accounting firm in Pittsburgh. I was twenty years old in my last year of college because I left a semester early to take a paid internship. I never got to enjoy my senior year the way some of my classmates did. They could go to the bars because they were twenty-one. I couldn't buy a drink with friends even after I entered the working world because I was still too young.

One of my accounting clients operated some nursing homes in Wadsworth. His comptroller was leaving, and he asked me to come to Ohio and work for him. He liked my work ethic. Even though I was an outside auditor, he noticed I wasn't afraid to work and put the time in at his offices, and I often arrived early and left late. I didn't want to go to Ohio at that time. Like my parents, I was happy living close to where I grew up. At the same time, I didn't want to upset my client. So, I thought I would outsmart him by making him a counteroffer he would certainly refuse. I told him that to leave Pennsylvania I would need to double the pay I was making at my current job. Oh, and I would also need a new car. My plan didn't work. I was shocked when he agreed to my terms. I didn't know what to do, but my dad gave me some advice that I never forgot. In fact, it would help shape all my future successes. "Once you give someone your word, you can never take it back," he said. "It's all you have in life." I was moving to Wadsworth, Ohio.

As I crossed the border into Ohio, the smokestacks of the steel mills and the coal mines receded. It felt like that moment in *The Wizard of Oz* when the black-and-white film turns to color. It seemed as if anything was possible in Ohio. The struggles I'd known growing up in Pennsylvania faded away. There were no mines and few mills — nothing but opportunity. People had jobs, the economy was growing. It seemed like a whole different world.

Soon after I moved to Wadsworth, I married Tina Teslovich, whom I first met in the sixth grade back in Saint Dominic Catholic School in Donora. We went to different junior highs, but we wound up at the same high school. The town was shrinking as work at the mills slowed, and several schools in the area merged. Tina and I started dating our senior year, and we continued to date while I was in college. We got engaged during my time working in Pittsburgh, and after the wedding, she moved to Wadsworth. We would go on to have three children in the years ahead.

The job that drew me to Ohio didn't turn out like I'd expected. I didn't realize my client's business was in serious trouble. Only after I got there and started working did I discover he owed years of back taxes. I was shocked, and at first, I worried if I'd made a terrible mistake. But walking into that mess and figuring out how to fix it was another important life lesson.

It took about a year to turn the nursing home operation around, and as I began to think about what I should do next, I decided that if my client could run nursing homes despite his tax problems, I should be able to do the same thing while learning from his mistakes. And I did learn a lot from him. He was an entrepreneur who took risks, made payroll and paid debt. At the time, I had about $200 in the bank. I filed my own incorporation documents and to pay the registration fee and cover some startup costs, I sold my 1980 Corvette, the first new car I'd ever owned. (A few years ago, I found it at an auto auction in Cleveland and bought it back. It had 12,000 miles on it when I sold it, and when I found it at the auction, it had only 30,000.)

At the age of twenty-four, I'd bought my first nursing home. I was now an entrepreneur taking risk, making payroll, employing people. Eventually, the business would grow to as many as 30 facilities, and a network of businesses that included a construction company and a health care services provider. I set up a consultancy for other nursing home operators, and ran companies that provided oxygen, as well as physical, occupational and speech therapy for patients. And I had my own accounting firm, which focused on the nursing home business. I also had a physicians' management practice that set up and designed physicians' offices. Basically, it was a large network of companies all focused on nursing and health care that employed more than 3,000 people.

By the year 2000, at the age of forty-two, I had sold most of the companies and begun looking for other things to invest in, including an amphitheater and some bars in Columbus. Over the next four years, I basically invested in a series of businesses such as bars, golf courses, restaurants — I was building a group of entertainment enterprises, much as I had built a group of interests around health care. In 2004, I partnered with businessman John McConnell, who owned the Columbus Blue Jackets professional hockey team. Together, we bought an arena football team in Buffalo, moved it to Columbus and rechristened it the Columbus Destroyers. About the same time, General Motors approached me about buying the local Chevy dealership in Wadsworth, which was struggling.

During this period, I also began my life in politics, starting at the local level. As I said, I grew up a Democrat, but I hadn't been too interested in politics during my business career, although I did believe in community service. I joined Wadsworth's volunteer fire department soon after I moved to town, and I served the department for almost five years. I still have a deep appreciation for firefighters and first responders, because few people realize how demanding the job is. Fires don't happen conveniently at 10:00 a.m. They happen at 2:00 a.m. There were times I fought a fire most of the night and then went to work the next morning. I had three young children, and I was spending all day at the office and running fires calls at night. I simply couldn't keep it up, especially as I got older. But my experience left me with an even greater respect for the people who help keep us safe.

As I became more well-known in the local business community, the mayor appointed me to the board of zoning appeals, and later to the planning commission. This gave me a taste of local government, and I began to do a little work for the local Democratic Party. The more work I did, though, the more I realized my beliefs — and the values I was raised with — no longer fit with the Democrats' increasingly liberal bent. I felt that the party was moving away from me. It wasn't the party that my grandparents or even my parents grew up with.

I voted for Ronald Reagan when he ran for president in 1980. His message of self-sufficiency resonated with me, as it did with so many other voters from both parties. By then, I was feeling that the Democratic Party had become the party of the handout, and Reagan believed in the handup, which I could relate to. As I grew my business, I began to identify more closely with the conservative agenda, and I embraced the Republican notion that the government should not be the ultimate solution for every problem. A few years later, I registered as a Republican.

As I was becoming more active politically and in the community, my fellow businessmen and women started to notice my accomplishments. They asked me to run for office. At first, I said no, but after several calls and requests I jumped into the race for city council president. I won, even though most of the city government was run by Democrats. The town was struggling with budget deficits, growth had stagnated, and the business community wanted to change things. Wadsworth was essentially a bedroom community, with little business base. Most residents worked in Akron or Cleveland. City leadership needed a business perspective, because expenses had gotten out of control, outstripping tax revenue.

As council president, I was essentially the vice mayor, and I worked closely with the Democratic mayor. I set the agenda for the city council for the next four years. When the mayor decided not to seek reelection, I ran for his seat and won. I made it clear I intended to serve only one term, long enough to get the city back on track financially.

I changed the way the city operated. In any deficit situation, a government has two choices: It can raise revenue or cut expenses. We knew we didn't need to raise taxes, but we did need to grow the economy. For far too long, the city had done too little to encourage growth and too little to keep expenses in check. The first thing I did was encourage development such as shopping centers at key intersections. Why not? Fifty thousand cars go by there a week. It was where development should go. We used public-private partnerships to pay for some of this and created tax increment financing. Sometimes, of course, a pairing of government and the private sector can end badly, but if done right and managed well, it can be mutually beneficial as we saw in Wadsworth.

Today, those intersections are bustling hubs of commerce — restaurants, home improvement stores, other retailers. By bringing in businesses, we were able to change the economic environment of the city and raise additional revenue.

Then, I took a look at the expense side. Quite simply, we were spending a lot of money that we didn't need to — things that had just sort of crept into operating procedures over time. For example, the fire department used to buy specific parts for its trucks from one local auto parts retailer. They'd been paying the same price for years. But we had several auto parts stores in town, so I suggested we shop around. We wound up getting parts costs down. A particular part that cost 31 cents now cost 7 cents. Why wouldn't we bid it out and get the best price? That's exactly what you'd do if you were looking for a part for your car at home.

I took some criticism. After all, the deal hurt the one parts store that had been marking up merchandise it sold to the city for years. But we took business and gave it to another local retailer that was willing to work for it. In the process, we saved the city — and the taxpayers — money.

These were the sorts of processes we needed to change, to make them more businesslike. Every contract had to have bids from at least two suppliers, and while we gave preference to local businesses, the price had to be competitive.

We made other common-sense adjustments, too. We sold off the city-owned vehicles that were used by many employees and replaced them with a mileage-reimbursement program. Our city is only about four miles wide. Providing some employees a vehicle just because they were department heads didn't make sense. That policy ended as well.

We also had an old recreation center that was costing the city about $1 million a year to maintain, and it was being used regularly by just a few hundred people. So, we took that $1 million a year and used it to build a new facility, which we then leased to the YMCA. Now, rather than all the citizens subsidizing a recreational facility that was used by a few people, the people who want to use it buy a membership at the Y. Today, the facility has three swimming pools, multiple basketball courts and state-of-the-art fitness equipment. Rather than costing the city money, it now generates revenue. What was a liability has become an asset.

Another big cost to the city was health care. We provided a great benefits plan at no cost to employees. Employees loved it, of course, but it resulted in added costs for the city, because even their spouses and other family members who had their own plans would sign up for the city plan. We were insuring a disproportionate number of family members, which is the most expensive type of coverage to provide. I made a slight adjustment. Employees would pay five dollars a month for an individual plan and $15 dollars for the family plan. It was far less than what other employees of other businesses were paying, but it was enough to make people consider other plans. We also bid out the insurance policy to multiple carriers, saving almost $500,000.

When I was elected, the downtown area had a high vacancy rate. We created a downtown Wadsworth group made up of civic leaders, and we started hosting events that were designed to draw people to the downtown area. As more people began returning to downtown, businesses came back, and we were able to restore the central corridor in town. Today, more than 95 percent of the downtown buildings are occupied. These sorts of programs don't cost money. It just requires us to conceptually change our thinking.

These decisions weren't politically driven. I still remember wondering why we had a part-time auditor making about

$60,000 a year but a staff that included a certified accountant doing all the work. The auditor was a Republican and a friend, but I still proposed cutting his salary in half. He wasn't happy, but he wasn't entitled to that pay. It was taxpayers' money. That's a problem in government at all levels: Elected officials spend money because it's not theirs. In the case of the auditor, I lost a friend, but I did what was right for Wadsworth. In all, during my tenure, I took a deficit of $1.5 million and turned it into a surplus without raising taxes.

We can apply the same formula to government at the state and federal levels: Cut out unnecessary expenses and find revenue sources to grow our economy. If we did the exact same thing I did in Wadsworth at the state and federal levels, those entities would be successful, too.

As my term came to an end, I began to look for what to do next. Wadsworth is a predominantly blue-collar town, and its economy is tied to the fortunes of manufacturing in nearby cities like Akron and Cleveland. By the mid-2000s, manufacturers across the Midwest were hurting, and that created a ripple effect in the local economy. Car dealers were particularly hard-hit. Wadsworth had three new car dealerships, and they were all getting slammed by the economic slowdown. I didn't know it at the time, but GM — at the government's direction, was about to administer a fatal blow.

🚗 🚗 🚗

A few days after I got the letter from GM informing me that the government was shuttering my dealership, I learned that some dealers had hired lawyers to contest the forced closings. But I also knew that fighting the government in court was likely to be futile. After all, the government had already overridden the legal process for bankruptcy and intervened in the business decisions of a private corporation.

I also heard that some members of Congress were actually talking about helping dealerships like mine that were run over by the GM and Chrysler bailouts — especially those members who had dealerships in their district. I contacted my congressman, John Boccieri, a recently elected Democrat. I had met him before through a friend, and he seemed like a nice guy when we talked on the phone about the dealership. He had replaced a Republican who had represented the district for thirty-six years. Boccieri met me in Wadsworth, I gave him a tour of my dealership, and, after hearing my story, he said he'd do what he could to help me.

We talked several times, and he vowed he would help me get my dealership back. About a month after I got GM's letter, several other representatives introduced a bill to reinstate the dealerships the administration wanted to close, and Boccieri promised to vote for it. I didn't know much about how Congress worked, but I appreciated his help, and I thought he was sincere.

On the morning of the vote, I sat down at my desk, turned on my computer and tuned in to the livestream of C-SPAN, eagerly waiting to see if my dealership and others would survive. Then I watched as Boccieri voted against the very bill he had told me he would support. I was furious. I called his cell and left him a message. I told him he couldn't be trusted. What I didn't understand at the time was the process. Democratic leadership in Congress had pressured him not to support the bill — to vote against his own constituents —in the name of party solidarity. I made Boccieri a promise of my own: "I'm going to do everything I can to remove you from office."

2

GETTING IN

I didn't know a lot about politics at that point, but I soon realized that nobody in the local political landscape had the strength to beat Boccieri. After all, he had the support of the president and many Democrats; even Vice President Joe Biden had attended his fundraisers in Washington and Ohio. Fortunately, thanks to that same administration, I found myself losing my car dealership, which gave me more free time and incentive along with it to challenge him. In addition, I had some money left over from my other businesses I could use to finance a campaign. So, in August 2009, two months after the government told me it was closing my business, I launched my race for Congress to represent Ohio's 16th District.

The district at the time was centered in Stark County, which includes Canton, home of the Pro Football Hall of Fame. At the time of the election, Stark voted solidly Democrat, although the district over the years had been a key bellwether in a swing state, and this congressional race soon attracted national attention. At the time, the district also included most of Ashland and Medina counties, as well as all of Wayne County. (Wadsworth is in southern Medina County, west of Akron.)

Within the four counties, few people outside of Wadsworth knew who I was, and even many of the party leaders knew little about me other than that I was a business guy and had been a small-town mayor. I faced three opponents in the primary. We all had to vie for the support of the party chairmen in each of the four counties. This is an area of politics that many people don't see. We talk about "grassroots" campaigning, but a campaign's success largely depends on the support you get from the local party infrastructure. I was a political novice. I thought that you threw your hat in the ring, ran the best campaign you could, and let the people decide. I didn't realize that the local party leaders could also put their thumb on the scale first. But I quickly realized that if I wanted to have a realistic chance of winning, I had to play the game.

I soon learned that the local party chairs wanted to get to know the candidates. They decided to set up a meeting on a Saturday that we were all asked to attend. Keep in mind, this was mid-2009, the advent of the Tea Party, and one of my opponents was about as far right as you can get. Much of his campaign centered on a promise that his first action if elected would be to introduce articles of impeachment against Barack Obama. Then, he would lead the charge to repeal the Affordable Care Act. Another opponent was about 70 years old and said he wanted to get into the race to change the thought process. A third candidate, who many saw as the favorite, was referred to by others in the party as the "golden boy." The Tea Party liked him, too. He had already run unsuccessfully in two primaries — one against the thirty-six-year incumbent, whom he almost defeated. Both were close races, which some in political circles believed gave him the automatic right to be the candidate this time around. He was clearly the favorite, and many people believed he had ambitions of higher office someday.

During that first interview, the chairman from Ashland County kept asking how much of my own money I was willing to put into the race. I guess I just didn't understand the rules. None of the other candidates had any personal wealth, so I knew he wasn't asking them that question. He kept pressing me to commit a specific amount of cash, and I finally said, "I'm going to put in whatever I have to put in to win, and let's just leave it at that. After a few more questions they thanked me and sent me on my way, telling me they would have a vote to decide who they would endorse. It was a little like what I imagine auditioning for a part in a movie must be like. Several weeks passed and I didn't hear anything, so I called the chairman of my county to find out what they'd decided. It turned out all they had decided was to have another meeting. That meeting, too, came and went, and then I called Jeff Matthews, the chairman of Stark County, which is the biggest county in the district. I didn't know Jeff at the time. He was a good guy who wanted to do what was best for his county, the state and, ultimately, the country. I told him I was getting ready to jump in the race, and I wondered if they'd made a decision. He told me they had decided to hold a third meeting.

I couldn't believe it. Not only were these local party leaders trying to influence the outcome of the primary, but they were holding up the entire process by not making a decision on how they wanted to influence the outcome. "Go ahead and have your meeting," I said. "I'm not coming. I'm done. You guys pick whoever you want. I'll see you at the primary." They had the meeting without me, and I later heard that three of the country chairs voted to support me and one voted to support the candidate from his county. It was my first lesson about the three Ls of politics: loyalty, location and largesse. But it was time to move on. I was all in.

I spent the next six months going around the four counties, shaking hands and talking with people, and I still think I surprised many voters because I did not act like a traditional candidate. I was a businessman, not a politician, and they didn't expect the hand-to-hand contact. Obviously, I'm pro-business, but not all my policies put business first. Given my background as a firefighter, I have always supported first responders, who in my district historically voted for Democrats.

I even attended a Christmas party at the home of one of my opponents. People were surprised to see me there, but I harbored him no ill will. Besides, my business career had taught me that sometimes the best way to win people's support is simply to go into the den filled with those who don't like you. After all, if I won the primary, I would need their support. And when I won, I'm happy to say that that opponent endorsed me in the general election.

The primary win was just the first step in an uphill battle. Now, I faced an incumbent who had been one of the top-five freshman congressmen and who was loved by President Obama. Our views, of course, differed greatly. He supported and voted for the cap-and-trade energy scheme to reduce greenhouse gas emissions, which was a centerpiece of Obama's "green energy" policies. No one in Ohio should have ever supported cap-and-trade, because the state is rich in natural gas, oil and coal, and it relies on those fuels to generate electricity. Add a complex bureaucratic trading scheme, overseen by the federal government, and the program would have required large manufacturers to buy carbon "credits," causing their operating costs to soar. Cap-and-trade wasn't just bad policy. It was a job killer for states like Ohio. But Boccieri voted for it for the same reason he failed to fight for my Chevy dealership: because his party's leaders wanted him to. He wanted to move up the ranks of party leadership, and you don't get to do that if you don't get on board with key policy initiatives.

Boccieri also was a key swing vote on the passage of "Obamacare," as the Affordable Care Act was commonly known. Obama was using all his political capital to ram health care reform through Congress, but at first, he didn't have enough votes in the House, even among the Democrats. Boccieri was one of five members who changed their votes from "no" to "yes," and Obama was grateful. In a speech in October 2010, less than a month before the election, Obama held a town hall meeting at George Washington University during which he praised Boccieri for supporting Obamacare even though it put his political career at risk. Obama came to Ohio several times during the campaign, speaking in cities like Youngstown and Parma, and each time he made a point of touting Boccieri. At a rally in Cleveland in late October, just days before the election, he appeared with Vice President Joe Biden and declared that Boccieri was "an outstanding young man, and we expect to send him back to Congress." The president, in other words, was doing everything he could to get my opponent reelected. A week before the general election, former President Bill Clinton came to town to campaign for Boccieri. This is what I was up against: an opponent who had the full support of the party in power.

I had support from my party, too, of course, but the chances of victory didn't look good. Unlike an incumbent, I didn't have a staff or extensive network of supporters to draw from. I had to build those from scratch. As modern campaigns go, mine was a low-budget, do-it-yourself affair. I had a 2004 Chevy Avalanche pickup, and I crisscrossed the district, driving myself to one campaign stop after another. I typically got in the truck at 7:30 a.m. and was on the road until 10:30 p.m.

One night, driving back to Wadsworth after a full day of campaign stops, I could feel myself getting more tired with each passing mile. The road began to blur in front of me, and although I needed to get home and get ready for the next day's campaigning, I also knew I was so tired I couldn't stay on the road any longer. I pulled off and slept for several hours before I awoke and drove the rest of the way home. I campaigned relentlessly because no one knew who I was or what I stood for, but gradually the tactics began to work. During one of my trips, I was in Canton, a Democratic stronghold, and I stopped at a Burger King in the middle of the afternoon. Behind the counter were three young, African-American women. One of them recognized me from a recent campaign stop. I wondered if she supported me. She called her co-workers over, introduced them, and asked for a picture. That's when I knew that the grueling campaign schedule was paying off and I was connecting with voters who might not have traditionally supported a Republican businessman.

While the personal attention was critical, so was my use of television. I had learned about the effectiveness of TV when I was helping to build the Arena Football League, and I had gotten comfortable in front of the camera. This is something many politicians have to learn. Some even hire coaches to help them appear more confident and relaxed. I took advantage of every media opportunity I could to get my name and my face on camera, and I spent as many dollars as I could on television ads. It wasn't vanity. I needed people to know who I was and what I stood for, and television has a reach that is greater than any other medium, including the internet. (While television may have helped me secure victory early in my political career, it would also ensure my defeat in my race for the Senate; but more on that later.)

In May 2010, as my campaign was gearing up, my contract with General Motors ran out, and I had to gather all of my employees together and tell them that my efforts to battle the arbitration process had failed. They all supported what I was doing, and some agreed to appear in my campaign ads. It was a stark reminder of why I was in the race. Later that day, I made a speech in Canton: "When the Obama administration first made clear its intention to take over General Motors and to dictate to small-business owners whether or not they could continue to operate privately owned businesses — which in some cases had been their family's livelihood for over 50 years, I feared we were witnessing one of the darkest days in American capitalism. And today, as I was forced to face my employees and tell them that we lost the fight and they've lost their jobs, it was clear that my fears were not misplaced."

The ties between Boccieri and the Obama administration drew national attention to the race. All the major networks had crews in the district throughout the campaign. As the campaign wore on, it was becoming clear that Republicans were going to win a large number of seats in Congress, and John Boehner predicted to a lobbyist I later got to know in Washington that he would become speaker of the House if I won my district.

The night of the election, I held what I hoped would be a victory party at The Galaxy, a restaurant and banquet center just off

Interstate 76 in Wadsworth (in one of the commercial develop-ments I had championed as mayor). All the networks were there, with their live trucks lined up in the parking lot outside. After the polls closed, several hundred people began showing up. I didn't realize it because I was huddled in a small room nearby with my staff, watching the returns.

By about 9:00 p.m., I knew that I had won. It's hard to explain the feeling when you win an election to federal office for the first time, especially in a tight race. There's less a sense of shock than a slow realization that you, a poor kid from a mining town in west-ern Pennsylvania, are now a member of Congress. It was a sur-real feeling, and it was still taking hold of me when Boccieri called about forty-five minutes later to congratulate me on my victory.

My wife, Tina; my mother; my sister; and my kids had gone out to the victory party about ten minutes earlier, and by the time I stepped through the door, the crowd was chanting "We want Jim! We want Jim!" The room erupted in cheers as I stepped to the podium.

I had defeated, by more than 20,000 votes, one of the golden boys of the Democratic Party, someone who had played basket-ball with the president at the White House. It was overwhelming. I barely remember giving my victory speech. It had been a brutal and expensive campaign. Various groups spent $6.3 million sup-porting me and Boccieri, and counting our own money and indi-vidual donations, it probably cost more than $15 million overall, making it the third-highest amount of any House race. Boccieri was one of five incumbents in Ohio who lost seats that night, and the state played a key role in helping Republicans retake the House. Of the ninety-four new representatives elected, eighty-five were Republicans. In the Senate, twelve of the thirteen new senators were from the GOP.

I was less concerned about what was happening nationally. In my acceptance speech, I hit on what would become the familiar themes of my congressional tenure — a balanced federal budget, bringing jobs back to the district and giving everyone a chance to achieve their American Dream just like I had some three decades earlier.

"We're starting to see a change because people are not happy," I said. "We've got to get our federal debt under control, and we've got to get jobs back into this district. When it comes to legislation, I'm going to make sure I read those bills. If somebody throws a 2,000-page bill on my desk, I'm going to throw it back at them."

The last line was a nod to Washington dysfunction that had already received a lot of media attention. The Senate bill for President Obama's health care reform was more than 2,000 pages long, and changes were made up until the night before the vote. Many of the lawmakers who voted for it hadn't read it. To me, reading what you voted for seemed like a logical first step toward reforming government. What can I say? It was my first race. I was a little naive.

Like many members of the Class of 2010, I came into the 112th Congress ready to change the world. The world, though, had other ideas.

3

REALITY SETS IN

I arrived in Washington on January 4, 2011, part of a wave of Republican freshmen who were eager to make changes and fix what we thought was wrong with Washington. I got to town a day before my swearing in, and I was greeted by a Marine who was waiting for my plane. Every new member of Congress got a personal Marine escort to the Capitol.

Walking into that building, staring up at the rotunda, I was again overcome by a sense of the surreal. I wasn't here as a visitor. I now worked here. This was part of my job. I have to say in the years that followed, through all the frustrations and battles I fought, I still felt a sense of awe walking up those Capitol steps. You can feel the history of the place envelop you. You are immersed in the very essence of our great experiment in democracy.

My family — my wife, my parents, my kids, my sister and brother-in-law, my two sisters-in-law and their husbands — and several friends and their wives arrived the next day, January 5. That morning, a mass was held at Saint Paul's, which we all attended along with John Boehner, the incoming speaker, and Nancy Pelosi, the outgoing one.

After mass, we went to the Capitol in time for my swearing-in ceremony in the House chamber. All the members are sworn in on the floor of the House, and then each member has a ceremonial picture with the speaker in which they stand, surrounded by their family, with their left hand on the Bible and their right hand raised.

The entire Capitol was abuzz. Each of us incoming freshmen felt we were part of something bigger. The people had spoken. They wanted something different, and we were going to make it happen. *Time* magazine declared us the "class to change America." Cameras were everywhere as the media tried to capture the moment. One news crew from Ohio even followed me as I walked around the Capitol and saw my new apartment for the first time.

After he was elected speaker of the House, my fellow Ohioan John Boehner gave a short speech that hit all the right notes:

"We gather here today at a time of great challenges. Hard work and tough decisions will be required of the 112th Congress. No longer can we fall short. No longer can we kick the can down the road. The people voted to end business as usual, and today we begin carrying out their instructions."

We wouldn't make good on any of it. We would fall short, we would kick the can down the road, and we would perpetuate business as usual.

To be honest, aside from that ceremony, much of those first two days felt like a family vacation. My parents were in their eighties by then, and I helped them get around the city, and then I hosted a dinner at a nice Italian restaurant for all my family, some close friends and a few others — about 17 people in all — who'd helped me during my campaign. It wound up being a bigger group than I'd planned, with lots of food and wine. When the bill came, it was $7,000. That same event in Wadsworth probably would have cost about $1,500. It was my first taste of what expenses were like in Washington, and it was a reminder that I was in a very different place from anywhere I'd worked before.

The day after the dinner, my family and friends went home, and I found myself sitting alone wondering, "Now what do I do?" It was really only then that the full weight of what had happened hit me. I was a member of the U.S. Congress. I would be doing things that Thomas Jefferson did and that Ben Franklin did, and that Abraham Lincoln did. It's an amazing feeling, and it's also daunting.

But I was also ready to get to work. After more than a year of following my campaign, the media continued to call on me. Reporters were used to me granting interviews, but now that I was in office, I had work to do. The people back home knew who I was; they had voted for me. I owed it to them to do my job, not keep getting my face on television. I told my communications director that I didn't want to do any more interviews until I had accomplished something worth talking about.

After going through the typical orientation for incoming congressmen, the House leadership assigned Steve LaTourette to be my mentor. Since 1995, Steve had represented Ohio's 14th and 19th districts, which cover the northeastern-most corner of the state. He was a Cleveland native and a former prosecutor who would leave office two years later because of the same dysfunction I soon would experience after a few years myself. By the time I arrived, he may have already been disillusioned with the place. He frequently railed against congressional shortsightedness on funding issues and he decried earmarks, the process by which lawmakers designate funding for pet projects in their districts, often at the expense of other, more worthwhile priorities. We were kindred spirits. (A year after leaving Congress, Steve was diagnosed with pancreatic cancer. He died in 2016 at age 62.)

Steve was well-liked by most of his fellow lawmakers and was known for being sensible and bipartisan. My first meeting with him was a bit of a shock. One week after I was sworn in, he called me over to his office in the Rayburn Building. I sat down in his office thinking he would share with me some insights into how to build consensus among my fellow congressmen or tricks for writing bills that could garner bipartisan support. Instead, he started the conversation by asking me, "Do you want to be happy here?" Like anyone starting a new job in a new field, of course I wanted to be happy. I looked at him, befuddled, and I finally said, "Absolutely, I want to be happy."

"Can you accept disloyalty and betrayal?" he asked.

I couldn't figure out where the conversation was going. It certainly wasn't what I expected for my introduction to federal office. I asked him what he was talking about. He asked me again if I could accept disloyalty. I said I wasn't sure anyone can. And then he asked again, stressing the word "you" — "Can *you* accept disloyalty and betrayal?" Finally, I said no.

"Well," he said. "You'll never be happy here then."

As shocking as it was, that conversation set the stage for my introduction to the realities of politics in our nation's capital. He went on to tell me that during my time in Washington I would find, on multiple occasions, that my friends and associates would betray my trust for their own benefit and political gain.

"That," he said, "is just Washington politics. So be prepared. If you can't accept that, then you're not going to be happy here."

🚃 🚃 🚃

As the new speaker of the House, John Boehner quickly found himself trying to control a large and unruly freshman class. He set up a weekly conference with us. We were a band of rebels, strong in our convictions and determined to fix what was broken with our government. At the start of the second day, Bob Goodlatte, a Republican from Virginia who was first elected in 1992, wanted to set the tone by having different representatives read the U.S. Constitution on the floor of the House. Debate quickly erupted over how to read it — should we include parts that had been nullified by amendment? So here we are, elected representatives sworn to uphold this grand document that forms the foundation of our government, yet we can't even agree on how it should be read.

Slowly, though, the political theatrics faded, and we began to get to work. First on our agenda: cutting spending and encouraging economic growth. Our first vote was a bill that cut 5 percent from our own committee and staff budgets. In the grand scheme of things, this wasn't going to eliminate the federal budget deficit. But it sent a message, and it made us sound a bit more credible when we turned our attention to other areas of the budget, which we fully intended to do. In fact, we vowed to vote weekly on bills that cut spending elsewhere. Many of us believed that we needed more of a business mindset when it came to federal budgeting and spending —- and there isn't a business leader anywhere who isn't looking to cut costs. Gradually, though, our determination would be worn down by the system.

Two weeks after my meeting with Steve, Speaker Boehner was handing out committee assignments. Although the speaker would never say this, he and the leadership team had a lot of authority on this process. In fact, I later learned that the same authority could be used to yank you from committee assignments, which was done to members who voted against leadership. Committees are where the real work of governing gets done. That's where legislation gets written, where it's debated, amended, and prepared for the vote by the full House. Or at least, that's how it's supposed to work.

I assumed my assignments would be based on my skills, experience and background, but that wasn't the case. As with the way most things operate in Washington, committee assignments don't follow a logical path. You don't necessarily get assigned to the committees you're most qualified for. Some committees have more political power than others, and these are the ones everyone wants to be on. A committee with a lot of power is a committee that makes it easier to fundraise and wield influence over other issues — and will attract the interest of even the most ill-prepared members of Congress. Then there are the committees that no one wants to be on, such as the Budget Committee. More on that in a moment.

All incoming freshmen submit their committee requests in writing. My top choice was Ways and Means, which is one of the more powerful committees because it oversees tax policy. I'd already been told I wasn't likely to get it, but I figured I'd come off a tough race and spent $1 million of my own money to get to Congress, so I might as well ask. My second choice was Financial Services, because during my years in business, I regularly interacted with banks and other money centers. Financial services had been instrumental in helping me build my companies. I knew firsthand that financing was critical to ensure business had access to capital. I wasn't sure how many of my fellow congressmen had ever applied for a business loan. My third choice was Energy and Commerce. Boehner gathered the Ohio delegation in his office and asked us what committees we wanted. He told us that as speaker, he couldn't show preference to fellow Ohioans, but he would do what he could to get us our preferred appointments. He went around the room. He pointed to Bill Johnson, who represented the 6th District and was sitting next to me. Johnson asked for Energy and Commerce. Boehner said no and told him he would be on Veterans Affairs. I chuckled to myself as Bill pressed his case. "Mr. Speaker," he said, "I really should be on Energy and Commerce. My district is rich with coal and oil." Boehner looked at him, took a long drag on his cigarette, and again said "Veterans Affairs." Bill was also new to Congress. He didn't realize how things worked. Then Boehner pointed at me. I said I wanted to be on Ways and Means.

"No freshmen get on Ways and Means," he said. This wasn't entirely true, but I knew it was a long shot, so I moved on to my second choice, Financial Services. By the way, some freshmen did get on Ways and Means that year. One had donated to the party to help others get elected. I guess that helped. But after I said Financial Services, Boehner said, "fine" and moved on to the next member.

A few days later, when the committee assignments were finalized, I was back in Ohio. I got a call from Steve LaTourette. He and Boehner were longtime friends and allies. Steve wanted to be chairman of the Transportation Committee, and Boehner passed him over a few years later, which was another reason he decided to leave.

But Steve started the call by saying, "Remember what I told you about disloyalty and disappointment?" he asked.

How could I forget?

"Well," he said, "it's happened already. You were promised Financial Services, but the speaker basically threw you under the bus and put you on [the] Agriculture, Transportation and Budget [committees] because he needed to move his agenda forward. He traded your seat for his benefit."

Steve told me he'd pulled Boehner aside after the meeting and told him, "You just fucked over Renacci." Boehner told him he had to.

I was stunned and furious. Agriculture? I had never been a farmer. I grew up in the shadow of western Pennsylvania steel mills. The closest I'd ever come to agriculture was driving past a cornfield on my way to Wadsworth. Not only was I angry that I wouldn't get to use my business skills on Financial Services, I also felt bad for the farmers. I had no understanding of the issues facing American agriculture. I felt my appointment was a disservice to the people who depended on farm bills and other legislation for their livelihoods, and it was an insult to me.

I asked Steve for Boehner's phone number, and he said he would give it to me, but I couldn't tell Boehner where I got it. After hanging up, I immediately began dialing the speaker's number. Before I could finish, my phone rang. It was a restricted number. It was Boehner. He apologized but said he had to do it. He didn't elaborate, but he promised to work to get me on Financial Services in the future. I give him credit for owning up to what he did, but I was still mad. It was my first lesson in how politics and the political agenda trumps policymaking.

Although I wasn't happy with what had happened, I knew that committees were important, and I planned to make my assignments the main focus of my work in Washington. If I and my fellow freshmen were going to change the way government operated, it would start with our committee work. I made sure I never missed a meeting — and that I arrived on time.

Fortunately, my stint on Agriculture, Transportation and Budget was short-lived. Later that month, Nancy Pelosi, who had been speaker and later, after the election, became the House minority leader, wanted to add another Democrat to the Financial Services Committee. Boehner agreed on the condition he also got to add a Republican. That enabled Boehner to honor his original promise to me. So I was finally on a committee where I felt I could do some good. I was put on the banking subcommittee (officially known as the Subcommittee on Financial Institutions and Consumer Credit), and soon after I joined, the vice chair, Kenny Marchant from Texas, was assigned to Ways and Means. I had gotten to know Marchant a little, and so I told him I would be interested in taking his vice chairman's seat. He offered to put in a good word for me. Then I went to the chair of the subcommittee, Shelley Moore Capito, and I told her I had a business background and would like to be her vice chair. She agreed and said she'd talk to Spencer Bachus, who was the full committee chair, and he agreed as well.

Bachus believed in letting the subcommittee chairs schedule their own hearings and allowed amendments to be drawn in the committee room. That's regular order — the process that the House is supposed to follow but rarely does these days. In fact, most committee chairs don't do this. Soon after I became vice chair, Moore Capito was recruited to run for the Senate in her native West Virginia (she was elected two years later, in 2014). Hitting the campaign trail meant she was twice as busy, which opened up an opportunity for me. I wound up chairing many of the hearings. It was a fantastic experience for a freshman congressman.

But I also saw the sham of committee leadership appointments. Technically, those committee chairmanships are supposed to be decided by committee members. In reality, the speaker controls that. Speakers want committee chairs who are loyal to their agenda, who they can work with and who can be counted on to play by the party's rules. This is true for both Republicans and Democrats, by the way — and yet another example of how Washington enforces firm control over process, even at the expense of good policy and representative politics.

It also creates a perverse system of personal ambition on the part of members of Congress. Many politicians spend their careers trying to get control of a committee. Working their way first into the chairmanship of a subcommittee, they plot their ascent to gain control of the full committee. When you're a committee chair, you get your picture painted and it will hang in the Capitol forever. Lobbyists will fill your campaign coffers with reliable frequency. Other members will do your bidding to get their own ideas for legislation a hearing on your committee. A chairmanship is the nearest thing in Washington to having your own empire. Except that these days, the empire must operate in the shadow of the House leadership.

As a result, committee chairs are not as powerful as they once were. After Newt Gingrich became speaker in the 1990s, power shifted to the leadership, which dictated what bills should make it to the floor. This was true through both the Republican and Democrat speakers who followed. They would often oversee the committee work personally, essentially looking over the committee chair's shoulder.

When I left Congress in 2019, some of my colleagues told me I was foolish, because I could have become a subcommittee chair on Ways and Means the next year. And I was leaving a committee that oversees all tax-related legislation. Ways and Means is one of Congress' most powerful committees, since no single law affecting the tax code can move forward without getting a hearing there. Given the way a few lines in the tax code can tilt the playing field in favor of one company or industry or even an individual, it's a committee that can reward its members with boundless power. But that's not why I ran for

Congress — to build power for myself. I came with a different purpose, and I wasn't going to stick around because I wanted a committee chairmanship. I was already blessed to have served as vice chair of the banking subcommittee, even if it was for only a short time and on the occasions when the chairwoman was not there.

🐘 🐘 🐘

If you were a kid growing up in the 1970s, you might remember "Schoolhouse Rock!"—the educational cartoons slipped in between the regular programs on Saturday mornings. One of the most famous was "I'm Just a Bill," in which an anthropomorphic piece of legislation sings a catchy tune that explains how he becomes a law in our system of government.

These days, Bill takes a very different path, and he rarely makes it into law. In the cartoon, Bill went through Congress like a young man on an adventure. Today, Bill would be better portrayed as a vagabond sitting on a park bench, ignored and unloved — one of society's forgotten.

That's not to say that bills never come to the floor of the House. That happens all the time, actually. If you look at the House, it's always passing bills. Each one has several sponsors, sometimes dozens of them. There are actually times when a bill has no co-sponsors. Those are ones that were written by the leadership and handed down to get on the floor. Those bills will become talking points in future meetings with voters and lines in political advertisements — Candidate So-and-So voted fourteen times for legislation that would fight crime, clean up the environment, cut taxes or whatever.

But most of these bills go nowhere further. Even if one party controls both the House and Senate, the Senate's rules make it far easier to block legislation from proceeding. And that happens all the time. Usually, Democrats only support bills from other Democrats, and Republicans only support bills from other Republicans. So, bills pass easily in the House because a simple majority can move a bill there. But the Senate's rules require sixty votes to move a bill, and when the country is divided like it is today, getting sixty votes is almost impossible. You may see a few members change sides, but it's rare. That's why John McCain's famous "thumbs-down" vote against the effort to repeal the Affordable Care Replacement in 2018 was so powerful. He bucked the Republican majority and prevented them from getting the sixty votes needed to move the bill to the president's desk for signing. Many Washington observers say that vote marked the end of the Republican majority in the House. We had lost our best chance to fix health care.

In the early days of the Tea Party, some lawmakers would cross party lines to vote their principles, but this can quickly cause you to run afoul of party leadership, so it doesn't happen often. McCain's vote put him at odds with party leaders, including the president, but he didn't care at that point. Besides, McCain had a reputation as a maverick.

All of these impediments contribute to a system in which bills pass, and bills die, and nothing changes. Legislation stagnates because we've short-circuited the legislative process. Hundreds of bills will pass the house on party lines. They often are nothing more than signature political statements that get passed on to the Senate to die.

Back in the "I'm Just a Bill" days, legislation had to have a certain number of co-sponsors to move out of committee. Committee members discussed the bill, added amendments and then presented it to the committee chair. Once the committee approved it, it was sent to the House floor, where there was open debate and, frequently, more amendments. The result was that a bill was thoroughly vetted by both sides. It was a process known as "regular order."

Today, the House leadership, usually the Speaker or the committee chair, huddles with a few like-minded colleagues in leadership to decide what bills will be passed. Committee members cloister themselves in separate meetings — Republicans in one room, Democrats in another. The path of legislation is charted before it ever leaves committee, and, in most cases, it comes down to a party-line vote. The process is so broken, it's like Humpty Dumpty fell off the wall and had his pieces scattered by a tornado.

Another thing that's broken in the process is hearings. You may see on the news that a particular committee was holding hearings, and you may think that means that the full committee assembles and hears from witnesses presenting both sides of an argument. The committee members then debate that information, find common ground, and craft legislation. But again, modern Washington is a world far removed from the quaint notions of "Schoolhouse Rock!" Today, the committee process is tainted.

Committee chairs, often in conjunction with their staff, and after approval from leadership, decide what hearings the committee will have. Once the topics are set, the majority gets to name three or four witnesses. The minority can name one. So, the majority party stacks the hearing with witnesses that will testify to what the majority wants to promote, and the minority view gets swamped. From the beginning, the outcome is a foregone conclusion.

For example, during my tenure on the Ways and Means Committee, we really believed we needed to have a hearing on a proposed border-adjustment tax, or BAT. It was a signature piece of the Republican tax plan, but no one on the committee even knew who engineered it or developed it. It just showed up as part of our Republican plan to move the country forward. A BAT is basically a value-added tax on imported goods. The leadership wanted to institute a BAT, even though some of us in the majority were opposed. We believed that such a tax would hurt ordinary Americans and the economy as a whole because so much of what Americans consume is imported. A tax on those imports would in effect raise the prices of everything Americans purchase. The Republican leaders asked us not to kill the tax, and then they presented four witnesses in the hearing who all supported the BAT. Now, some of the biggest retailers in the country opposed the BAT, but we didn't hear from industry leaders. Some business groups and trade associations opposed the BAT, but we didn't hear from them, either. Instead, we heard only from carefully selected supporters.

The problem was that even the one witness who did speak against the tax was basically drowned out by the four who spoke in favor. It's human nature. If you hear four people applauding a measure and one person denouncing it, you're more likely to think that most people support it. And when people see the hearings on television, and they see most of the witnesses espousing one point of view, it tends to sway public opinion as well. The BAT hearing didn't go well for the House leadership. Several of us on the committee didn't support the BAT. I had said behind closed doors that I opposed it. If four Republicans voted against it, the tax would die in committee. The committee chair asked me to keep silent during the hearing. He didn't want me stirring up more opposition. It turns out, I didn't have to. To my surprise, three others on the committee asked questions in opposition. I asked one yes-or-no question to all of the witnesses: Will the BAT raise prices for consumers? They all said yes. The next day, one of the Washington papers wrote: "Regarding the BAT, Renacci fired the kill shot." All I did was raise a simple question that too often gets forgotten: How does this legislation affect the people we represent?

At the very least, the number of witnesses for and against an issue should be equal. But then lawmakers would have to do the hard job of actually studying an issue and making a decision based on what's best for the country, rather than what party leaders tell them is best for the party.

While on the Ways and Means Committee, we held weekly but separate lunch meetings for Republicans and Democrats. I always thought it would have been better to have all the members gather for one lunch. Sure, we would have had our disagreements, but we also would have gotten to know each other, which would have made it easier to work together. Instead, we huddled in our own camps, and then when the full committee would meet for a hearing, you had the two sides squaring off. Instead of listening to the witnesses, gathering information and making informed decisions, most full committee meetings quickly devolved into partisan carping, with each side taking shots at the other. The public sees all the displays of divisiveness, but behind the scenes, it's worse: Most Democrats and Republicans barely care enough to even argue with each other. That was something I was going to try to change.

4

BIPARTISANSHIP IS NOT A DIRTY WORD

About a year after I was elected, I was invited to a dinner at the Italian Embassy with other Italian-American members of Congress — about seven Democrats, myself, and one other Republican, fellow Ohioan Pat Tiberi. We had a little wine, some good food and a lot of fun. As the dinner wound down, one of the Democrats invited me to the National Democratic Club. I thought he was half-joking, but he was serious. I didn't even know there was a National Democratic Club, but in Washington each party has their own social club that functions almost like a social safe place. You can go there and relax without worrying about running into a member of the opposition or the press. I looked over at Tiberi, who had been in Congress for about sixteen years at that point, and he said, "No Republican ever goes to the Democratic Club." He'd never been there himself. I wasn't planning to go, but I needed a ride back to Capitol Hill. As I came out of the embassy, Bill Pascrell, a friend and Democrat from New Jersey, offered to give me a ride. As I got in, I realized we weren't alone. Mike Capuano of Massachusetts, Mike Doyle of Pennsylvania, and John Larson of Connecticut were all in the car. It was a tight fit, and I was the only Republican. "You're coming to the Democratic Club with us," Pascrell said. There was no turning back.

It turns out the Democratic Club is not far from my old office in the Canon Building, and it's right around the corner from the Republican Club. When I walked in, it was like something out of a movie. Everything seemed to freeze, but just for a second. Marsha Fudge, a congresswoman from Ohio, greeted me along with others. The Democrats welcomed me into their safe place. Representatives and senators were sitting around drinking and watching television, and they all stopped and looked at me. One of them finally said, "Renacci, what are you doing here? Republicans don't come in here." I shrugged and said, "Well, I'm in here now," and I went and sat down. I must say, they treated me like royalty. The manager of the club came over and offered me food and drink.

Everyone treated me like a friend. I think the others in the club appreciated that I was willing to even walk in the door. About twenty-five minutes later, Tiberi showed up and came over to me. "Pascrell told me you were here," he said, looking around nervously. "Nobody ever comes here." But I did, and it was one of the best bipartisan times I had in Washington. I wound up being invited to the Democratic Club probably twenty or thirty times over the next few years. They'd wave me in like Norm on "Cheers," and I'd sit down, watch TV, and enjoy being with them as friends rather than people from the "other side." Doyle, who was from Pittsburgh, invited me one night to watch the Penguins play a Stanley Cup series game. He knew I was a Penguins fan. Heck, I tried to buy the team at one point with an investment group. As we watched, you couldn't tell who was a Republican or Democrat. You could only tell who was a fan and who wasn't. We had a lot of fun, and I formed genuine friendships in that club that continue to this day.

And I reciprocated. On several occasions, Tiberi and I invited some of our friends from the Democratic Club to the Republican Club. But I have to admit, the food at the Democratic Club was better. It wasn't just club-swapping, either. I went to a number of "Democratic events." Derek Kilmer of Washington state invited me to the premiere of one of the "Star Wars" movies that he had set up as a fundraiser. I was the only Republican in the entire theater. I was also invited to the Democrats' annual Christmas breakfast one year, and I attended a fundraiser for John Carney of Delaware when he ran for governor.

We were friends, and while we didn't agree on everything, we did agree on civility and friendship. During one of the debates in the Ways and Means Committee over the president's tax returns, Pascrell called me stupid. I walked over to him during a break and I said, "You called me stupid." He smirked and said, "You are stupid." We both laughed. I knew he didn't mean it. It was what politics do to people.

I refused to adhere to the unspoken — and sometimes outspoken — rule that I shouldn't be seen in the presence of Democrats. I found the partisan intransigence I saw on display at almost every turn in Washington stifling and counterproductive. From the moment I arrived, I worked to do something about it. It didn't take long for me to realize that bipartisanship was not dead. Below the leadership level, many members of Congress wanted to work together. But most were under so much pressure from the leadership that they couldn't.

In January 2011, I went to my first meeting of the Financial Services Committee under Spencer Bachus. He gave everyone five minutes for opening statements. I've said that nothing in Washington starts on time, but Spencer was the exception. He scheduled a 10:00 a.m. hearing, and he was in his chair five minutes early. At exactly 10:00 a.m., he would gavel the meeting to order, and if you were in your seat, you got to go ahead of everyone who was late, regardless of your seniority. Typically, in a committee that size — there were 33 Republicans — freshmen might not get a chance to speak. But under his rule, showing up on time meant you might, even if you were a lowly freshman. It was a great policy, and I always made sure I was in the room ten minutes early.

Of course, he couldn't do much about what was said, and that first hearing of mine followed the path of so many others that would come after it: A Republican took five minutes complaining about the Democrats; then a Democrat took five minutes complaining about the Republicans. And so it went. When Bachus recognized me, I said: "Look, I know I have five minutes, but I'm not going to take them. Here's the problem: I didn't come here to Washington because I wanted to sit for now almost an hour and listen to the Democrats throw stones at the Republicans and the Republicans throw stones at the Democrats. We have some witnesses down here. I'd really love to hear from them. And that's what we should be doing." And I yielded the rest of my time.

Everyone was shocked. After the hearing, John Carney, who was then a freshman Democrat from Delaware (and now the state's governor), walked over and told me he appreciated what I said. He said he felt the same way and wanted to know if we could sit down over breakfast. We got together a few days later and talked about the things we had in common: the reasons we came to Washington, our desire to get things done and the importance of working together. At the end of the meeting, we agreed to each find a few others who shared these principles and bring them to another breakfast meeting. For the next meeting, we had about six people, and the meeting after that we had twelve. We started having a regular bipartisan breakfast at 7:30 a.m. on the first morning of the session. As the year went on, we realized that members have so many meetings, fundraisers and other demands on their time that it was hard for them to make every breakfast. But we believed the breakfast was important, so we set down a few rules. The first was that everyone had to make 70 percent of the meetings if they wanted to continue being invited. Another was that whatever was discussed in the room had to stay in the room unless three-fourths of the attendees agreed to make it public. Our concern was that if people shared our discussion with the press, our respective party leadership might get upset and shut us down. But the overriding purpose remained the same: We would work together to move our country forward.

Of course, as things progressed, and the number of fundraisers increased, attendance began to trail off. What started as a bipartisan breakfast of six Republicans and six Democrats might have only half that many at any particular meeting. So, we found more potential members — a total of thirteen on each side —

which meant that at any one meeting, we might have between twelve and sixteen representatives total.

Other than John and me, no one prioritized the meeting, so fundraisers and other demands kept getting in the way. But we had good discussions regardless of who showed up, and we started to bring in speakers to talk about different issues. Over time, the breakfasts became a core group of people who could work together, who liked each other, and who had common ground.

And it made a difference. Most of the bills I sponsored or co-sponsored had bipartisan support, and the reason was simple: I had made friends on the other side and we learned to trust each other. We passed fifteen bills out of the House, and seven became laws. They included a bill to give states more flexibility on reimbursements that businesses receive for unemployment insurance, several aimed at curbing identity theft, and one that gave the Internal Revenue Service the authority to fire any employee who used their position for political purposes.

Meetings like our breakfast are really the answer to a lot of the problems we have today in Congress. It's as simple as finding a core group of people in the middle who can come together in spite of the divisions that define our politics. The far right holds together and busts up the right side of our body politic, and the far left holds together and busts up the left side. But if people from both sides can come together in the middle, it can offset the pressure from the extremes on both sides.

🁢 🁢 🁢

Why, you may wonder, can't others in Congress find similar ways to bridge their differences? It's become common to talk wistfully about the days when members of the two parties could work together and, in some cases, even be friends. Ronald Reagan had genuine affection for Tip O'Neill, the Democratic House Speaker during his presidency. What's changed?

Lots of things, of course. Politics has always invoked strong feelings, but today, things are different, and worse. For one thing, people are much more likely to equate their politics with their personalities, and they think people who disagree with them aren't just misguided but also evil. So much of our politics is cultural and geographical. People surround themselves with others they agree with and who share lifestyles that comport with their own. They consume media and entertainment that further validates their own views, so they never challenge themselves to understand an issue from another person's point of view. Meanwhile, our politicians are becoming celebrities, the modern equivalent to spiritual leaders. Look at the fanatical throngs that rally around Beto O'Rourke, Bernie Sanders or, yes, even Donald Trump, and you can see groups of people who revere their candidates like rock stars rather than public servants.

Social media has added to the divide. Nothing has to be true on social media; it just has to get clicks. Clicks mean attention, and the more attention, the more the conventional media covers you. I passed a bill with John Lewis, the longtime Democratic congressman from Georgia, to help end identity theft. That should have been big news, but it got swallowed on social media by the latest bluster over some issue from the far left or far right flank.

But there's also a more mundane reason for today's divisions: earmarks. When we took earmarks out of the budget process, we shut down the system that allowed members to request federal money for public works projects and other programs in their districts. It was, on one level, a smart move because it forced members of Congress to justify spending every taxpayer dollar on the merits. But it turned out to have a terrible outcome: It reduced the need for people in Congress to work together.

If you travel the country, you will see signs of earmarks from decades past. These were pet projects that members of Congress championed for their districts. Some were a waste of money;

others weren't. Some, of course, were used as a way for members to get reelected. Ralph Regula represented my district for 36 years, and if you travel around northeastern Ohio, you'll see the Ralph Regula Post Office, the Ralph Regula Justice Center and a bridge over Route 77 welcoming people into Stark County. He spent years on the Appropriations Committee, and those were earmarks that he "brought home" for the district.

In the old days, a congressman would approach the Appropriations Committee and say, "I need $1 million for a bridge in Wadsworth." If he was Republican, and the Democrats were in charge of the committee, they would say, "Well, we'll give you that $1 million for the bridge in Wadsworth, but we need you to support a $3 million parking and recreational center in this other district. Let's work together." It created a financial quid pro quo. As I'll explain in the next chapter, we weren't following the proper budget process then either, and the earmark negotiations served as a shortcut to a shortcut. The only way a congressman could get federal funding for local projects was to cut a deal with earmarks.

Earmarks came under increasing criticism as wasteful spending. The end came in 2005, after the late Senator Ted Stevens and representatives from Alaska pushed for $223 million in earmarks for a bridge connecting the Alaskan town of Ketchikan to its airport on neighboring Gravina Island. After coming under fire from other members, the proposed earmarks were rescinded. As governor, Sarah Palin eventually canceled the project, which became known as the "bridge to nowhere." It was a powerful image, and it instilled in the minds of voters of both parties just how out of control the earmarks game had gotten.

Now, sadly, earmarks are still in the system. But the president decides where all the money goes. Money is spent in each district at the whim of the administration, and then the representative writes a press release proclaiming what he or she did for the district. But it's not their decision, and it's not like the old days when they had to fight and fight and fight to bring money back home. Even worse, depending on the party in power, those earmarks can be used to help candidates get elected. When I was running for my second term against Betty Sutton, President Obama earmarked dollars for the district. Of course, she claimed she brought them home, but that wasn't how the process really worked.

It's not a coincidence that the rise of discord in Washington coincides with the end of earmarks. Don't get me wrong, I supported eliminating the old quid pro quo system, but earmarks could also be a good thing, as long as they could stand on their own merits. If a bridge is collapsing on an interstate highway in Missouri, then the government should step in to fix it. But the representative should make the case in public, so that everyone can see how much is being spent. That might actually reduce the partisan bickering, because members would need one another's support to win funding. But earmarks will never come back because the opposing party will hammer the earmark recipient in the media. When Paul Ryan was elected speaker in 2015, several members talked about bringing them back. He said we couldn't make that a priority and warned that it could cause us to lose the majority. I'm not sure it was the right call. We wound up losing the majority anyway.

I consider myself in most cases a loyal Republican, but I found the lack of willingness to work with the Democrats frustrating. It was more than just the zero-sum game of political one-upmanship that seemed to always be raging on Capitol Hill. It was the pervasive us-versus-them mentality that had come to define us not as representatives but as people. We weren't supposed to associate with the other side, as if brushing against a Democrat would give us some incurable disease and cause us to vote for Obamacare.

Our system of democracy is built on compromise, and that means working with people you disagree with. You can still find common ground, and you can still enjoy their company.

Our bipartisan breakfasts continued for eight years, and other groups are still trying to carry on the tradition today. Unfortunately, finding representatives who seek the middle ground is the easy part. The problem is when the party leadership gets involved. I used to go to Republican leaders and tell them that I had twelve or fifteen Democrats who come to meetings all the time and who want to get things done.

I urged the leaders to come to the meeting and talk to them. They said they would, but they never did. During the Syria crisis in 2016, I was one of several Republicans invited to the White House by President Obama, who wanted our backing. Obama, as I had heard happened many times, didn't show up for the meeting, but Vice President Joe Biden did. Afterward, I told him, "It's interesting that you call us over here and ask for our help, but you never come talk with us any other time." I mentioned that I co-chaired the bipartisan breakfast, and that I'd love for him to attend. He told his staff he wanted to go, but he never did. There were always scheduling conflicts. The only individual in leadership who came to the breakfast was Kevin Brady of Texas, when he was leading the negotiations for the tax bill in 2017. I give him credit for coming, but it wasn't a social call or a desire to spread bipartisanship. He, like Obama, wanted our support for his bill.

Republican leaders in the House told me that while it was great that I was trying to work with the other side, the Democrats would never cross over and help us when we needed them to. Talking to Democrats, they said, was a waste of time. The Democrats might say they want to help get things done, but when it came to needing their vote, they would just vote the party line. It might have been true, but I believed that nothing would change if we didn't try. I'm sure the same was said on the other side. What was lacking was leaders who wanted to grow the middle by working with both sides. Too often, the leadership pressured members of our group to vote along party lines. We might have had great relationships, and we might have struck agreements and shook hands on it, but when it came to the vote, and we had to face pressure from our respective leadership, many of our members changed their minds. That's why I'm proud of the bills we were able to pass, because it showed that it was possible to work together.

5

COMMITTEE
OF THE DAMNED

I may have been one of the few members who liked serving on the Budget Committee. As I mentioned, no one wants to be involved in budgeting because you have to take some votes on a budget or amendments that never get passed anyway. Your votes are on the record, and they're used against you by your opponents in political ads. But it's disingenuous — and irresponsible — to just say, "Let's raise the debt to $22 trillion." You have to at least attempt to rein in spending and attack the deficit. Most lawmakers may say they want to cut the deficit, but no one wants to curtail spending on the projects or programs voters tend to like. No one in Congress ever says, "this is good, we need this, but we can't afford it, so we're not going to do it" unless it's the other party's project. As a result, the Budget Committee is filled with freshman congressmen, all trying to get off of it as quickly as possible. I may have been the exception. I wound up serving on the committee off and on over the eight years I was in Congress. In fact, I believe everyone should have to serve on the Budget Committee for at least one term so that they realize our spending issues.

I didn't know much about how the federal government did its budget when I started, but I was a Certified Public Accountant and had a lot of experience looking at balance sheets, income statements and other tools of the budgetary trade. I took the job seriously, but when you're trying to work up the federal budget, you quickly run into big challenges.

Before the Class of 2010 came into office, when the Democrats controlled the House and Nancy Pelosi was the speaker, the Budget Committee simply stopped doing budgets. The Democrats realized that any attempt at balancing the budget would require spending cuts, and they didn't want to do that. Instead, they did nothing. Then, the Republicans swept in and before long they adopted the same do-nothing approach.

Budgeting used to matter more because it had a more direct impact on spending. Discretionary spending used to represent the largest portion of the budget. Discretionary programs are everything except interest payments and entitlements — Social Security, Medicaid and Medicare. Most of that spending is pre-determined by law and really can't be altered unless Congress makes major changes to the programs and the law. Today, 70 percent of the budget is mandated by entitlement programs and interest. Another 15 percent is military spending, which is technically discretionary, but as a practical matter, no one wants to cut it for fear of being branded un-American. The result is that any budget Congress passes represents only about 15 percent of all federal spending. You could pass a budget that had no discretionary spending at all and it wouldn't make a significant impact on the deficit. So, Congress basically decided it wasn't worth the trouble.

To understand how broken the budgeting process has become, it helps to understand how the process is supposed to work. The federal budgeting process is supposed to have five steps:

1. Federal agencies submit their spending proposals to the president, often a full year ahead, for the fiscal year that will start on October 1. The president and his budget team review them, set their own priorities, calculate the revenue that they expect to receive in the coming year and then draft a budget request and present it to Congress in February.

2. The budget committees in the House and Senate hold hearings and then write their own budget resolutions and vote on them. These resolutions set the outlines of a budget — how much will be taxed; how much will be spent and how much new debt the nation will accrue. The decisions about how much will be spent on individual programs go to the House and Senate Appropriations Committees (this is why this committee was so sought after — it got all the glory and got to spend all the money).

3. The twelve appropriations subcommittees in each chamber then determine the amount of spending that's allowed for

all discretionary programs. This process is often referred to as the markup.

4. When that work is complete, the budget goes back to the full budget committees in the House and the Senate, where members debate and vote on the appropriations bills. Then the bills go to the floor of both chambers, where they are amended and, presumably, approved one by one. This should be a long process and probably some of the most important work that Congress does. But most years it's simply ignored.

5. Then each approved appropriations bill is sent to the president to sign. After the president signs all twelve bills, the budget process is complete. That's supposed to happen before the start of the fiscal year.

In reality, none of this happens. One of the reasons why the federal government is always threatened with a shutdown is because the federal budget is like an unloved dog that nobody wants to take care of in Washington. Any problem in our politics gets taken out on the budget process — whether we're talking about taxes, deficits, funding our troops, paying for a border wall or keeping IRS refund checks rolling — the root cause was our failure to pass a budget properly and on time.

How we got here is actually a pretty good story, and one that's often overlooked. Back in 1973, amid the many battles he was dealing with at the time, including the Watergate investigations and hearings, President Richard Nixon squared off with Congress over budget deficits. Nixon demanded that Congress cap spending at $250 billion a year and threatened to veto any appropriations bills that helped exceed that amount. Then, when Congress ignored his veto threats, he invoked a presidential power known as impoundment to set aside tens of billions of dollars, essentially defunding programs he didn't like. Other presidents had used impoundment, but never to such a degree. Nixon claimed the Constitution gave him the right to decide whether to spend the money. But that wasn't right. The Constitution gives Congress the "power of the purse." The details on how that power would be exercised were left unclear, and Nixon was trying to take more of that power for himself.

Congress passed the Congressional Budget and Impoundment Act of 1974 precisely to limit Nixon's (and future presidents') control of the budget process. The bill created the Congressional Budget Office as well as the Budget Committees and implemented a budgetary process that left the president with far less wiggle room. With this law, Congress got to use the president's proposed budget as a starting point, but then took over the analysis and discussion of the nation's priorities. The president can stay involved and still has to sign the budget into law, but the president no longer has the right to override the explicit direction of the budget passed by Congress.

But the catch is this: While Congress took a lot of power away from the White House, it also took on a lot of responsibility — including the responsibility to get its budget work done on time. If Congress were doing its job, it would pass a budget by February or March each year, and the appropriations committees would work on getting their respective bills done by September. Then, when the new fiscal year starts on October 1, you would have twelve appropriations bills that all tie in to that budget. The president would have to follow whatever was appropriated, and, as a final step, the House would authorize the budget. So, the process should be budget, appropriate, authorize.

But over more than four decades, this process has never worked as designed. The CBA, as the law is known, was supposed to set parameters to ensure federal spending came in on time and within the budget. The very first budget resolution under the law, in 1975, came in a month late and set spending higher than President Gerald Ford had requested. It's only gotten worse since then.

The absence of a budgetary process is precisely the kind of thing most Americans should understand about Washington. It's no shock that the nation has a long wish list of spending items — everybody knows that. In fact, most businesses and households live with that reality every day. What's shocking is that while most businesses and households would prioritize their wish lists in a budget — separating their "need to have" lists from "want to have" lists — Congress really doesn't bother. The budget process as we experience it at home does not exist in Washington. It's more like a situation where nobody agrees on where the limits are, nobody agrees on the priorities, and nobody is held accountable when more debt gets loaded on the nation's credit card. After more than forty years of this, nobody (at least in Washington) even thinks it's unusual or particularly scandalous. It's absurd, and we shouldn't be surprised by what's happened: Since the CBA's passage, Congress has adopted a budget resolution only six times, the national debt as a percentage of gross domestic product has more than tripled, and Congress has run deficits in 39 of the past 45 years.

Here's how things "work" now: Typically, we don't bother passing a budget. If the House passes one, then the Senate doesn't, or vice versa. There's no agreement on what the budget should be. Sometimes appropriations bills get done; sometimes they don't. Instead, we bypass the first two steps in the process, budgeting and appropriations, and we go straight to authorizing. But how can the government authorize trillions of dollars in spending when it hasn't even tried to do a budget?

Good question. Again, never underestimate the creativity of a body of legislators who can write their own rules. When Congress started making a habit of bypassing the normal budget process, it invented a gimmick called the continuing resolution, or CR.

CRs were another provision of the 1974 budget law, and as designed, they were kind of innocuous. They were supposed to provide temporary funding for federal agencies in case there was a delay in voting appropriations bills into law. A CR extends the existing appropriations bills until a specific date. It's basically saying: "We'll allow these agencies to spend money this year as if it were last year — same levels, same programs, same everything." A CR allows federal agencies like the Veterans Administration, the Department of Housing and Urban Development, or the Agriculture Department to keep spending money on programs without congressional intervention or control.

During my eight years in Washington, we did more than 20 CRs. I voted against all of them except one. The reason is simple: CRs pass all spending control back to the president. It's basically handing the president a checkbook and telling him that he has, say, $3 trillion in the account and he can spend it however he wants. That's why President Obama and later President Trump could make seemingly random spending decisions. Congress has basically abdicated its responsibility for budgeting and given all the power to the president. That way no one in Congress has to take the heat for difficult budgeting decisions, and the party in power shows its "support" for the president by handing him more financial power than he's supposed to have. Budgeting, as anyone in business can tell you, is about making tough choices. The process, as it exists today, removes that responsibility from Congress and makes it a political football. And we know what the result is — bloated deficits, runaway federal debt and repeated government shutdowns. In fact, the long-running 2013 government shutdown was the result of a fight over a CR.

Remember my second rule of government dysfunction: No one has a budget. This is why it matters. If no one has the financial discipline to set a budget and follow it, the federal finances just continue to deteriorate. How can Congress expect to make effective policy if it doesn't understand how much it can spend? The seeds of government inefficiency are sown in the absence of budgets.

The complexity of the federal budget lends itself to gamesmanship. Back in the late 1990s, Bill Clinton made a big deal of balancing the budget. But the budget that the Clinton administration proposed in the late 1990s, for example, actually increased spending by $10 billion and the deficit for that year was initially projected to be $120 billion, which back then seemed like an insurmountable hole to close. But it did close, thanks to massive unexpected tax revenues generated by the dot-com stock market boom. So, yes, I appreciate that President Clinton oversaw the surplus of the late 1990s, but he backed into it. The point is that the budget was balanced in spite of Washington's lackadaisical approach to finances, not because lawmakers finally found fiscal discipline. It was pure luck, but don't think a president — Republican or Democrat — won't take credit for that kind of luck.

If there were any lessons to be learned from Clinton's so-called surplus, they were quickly lost. In fact, we've had efforts over the past thirty years to rein in spending — the Gramm-Rudman-Hollings Balanced Budget and Emergency Deficit Control Act of 1985, the Balanced Budget and Emergency Deficit Control Reaffirmation Act of 1987, the Budget Enforcement Act of 1990, the Balanced Budget Act of 1997, the Budget Control Act of 2011 — but all have failed. And then we pretty much stopped trying. The government has operated in deficit since 2001.

Consider the fiscal 2016 budget. We Republicans claimed that it balanced the budget, without the surge in tech revenue that helped Clinton. But we played games with the numbers, too. We assumed that tax reforms would generate $1 trillion in revenue (they didn't) and that Obamacare would be abolished, which would trigger an economic boom that would boost revenue (it wasn't, and it didn't).

Part of the reason the deficit continues to grow is that we basically reverse engineer the budget. Under the current system, realistic budget numbers would make everyone's assumptions explode.

For example, tax cuts rarely produce the economic growth and revenue expected and promised. At the same time, government programs rarely cost as little as expected, and they grow in scope forever (Ronald Reagan famously said that the nearest thing to guaranteeing eternal life is to become a government program). The only way you can make the numbers appear to work is by making wild assumptions that everyone knows are either untrue or unlikely. Just like with entitlement programs, the longer we refuse to reform the budgeting process, the more the numbers move against us. If you're frustrated by what I've just described, just wait. We haven't gotten to the most-alarming part.

As I mentioned, most of the budget — and the deficit — wouldn't even be touched in the budget process. Even if the budget process existed, we still wouldn't discuss roughly 85 percent of what the federal government spends every year. This is the part that is set aside for interest payments, entitlements and the military. When Medicaid, Medicare and Social Security were created, they were set up as transfer programs, funded by their own dedicated income streams (FUTA, FICA and those other abbreviations on your paycheck are your share of those costs). Those programs' current and future costs are driven almost entirely by demographics — how many people retire each year, for example. The only way for Congress to control those programs' costs is to pass laws that, in the hands of a half-decent political ad maker, sound horrendous. If, let's say, you want to limit the growth of Social Security by lowering the rate of growth in Social Security payments from 3.1 percent to 2.7 percent, you'll soon see your opponent running ads targeting you for "wanting to cut Social Security." It doesn't matter that Social Security payments will still be rising and that these payments are for current workers who won't be retiring for decades. You will be the devil pushing grandma off a cliff. I've seen it happen too many times.

If politics didn't get in the way, both parties would admit the need to make tough decisions on these programs and work together to find a solution, however difficult. But it's far easier to keep ignoring the problem and attack members of the opposing party for offering up solutions. It's also the best example of Washington's prevailing strategy: Kick the can down the road and hope you're not still there when it implodes.

Medicare, Medicaid and Social Security are the greatest threat to the long-term financial well-being of the country, but under the current laws you can't touch them. Those laws would have to be changed by the same people who want to be reelected, which won't happen if they share these facts honestly with their constituents.

As for the interest expense on the federal debt, that's intractable, because it's money we must pay in the present and the future for spending too much in the past. All these requirements — interest, entitlements and the military — leave us to battle over just 15 percent of the budget, but we can't even keep that under control.

Sadly, entitlement programs are an analogy for all of the government's financial troubles. If you don't address the biggest issues — ones that everyone knows represent a looming crisis — how can you deal with the more mundane budgeting realities? As a result, our government spends more every year than it takes in. When lawmakers talk about "cutting spending," it may seem as if they want to tighten their belts. After all, when you talk about saving money in your household budget, you might decide to eat out less or skip going to the movies. But Congress has put almost $22 trillion on its credit card, and that doesn't include its unfunded liabilities for programs such as Social Security, Medicare and Medicaid.

For the 2019 fiscal year, the government budgeted total spending of $4.4 trillion, even though it estimated it would receive about $3.4 trillion in revenue, which is still an astounding sum of money. Because nobody seems to pay the price for such deficits (except, of course, future generations), nobody is willing to take the political hit for bringing them under control. For fiscal 2020, President Trump submitted a $4.7 trillion budget request, despite projections that trillion-dollar deficits would persist for four years. In simple terms, our government is living beyond its means, and it has been for decades, through both Republican and Democratic control of the White House and Congress.

When I arrived, I was too naïve or blind to see the hopelessness of the situation. I saw a problem, and I had some ideas for a solution. As a businessman, I had the experience that I thought would help Congress rein in this problem. How logical I was ... and how foolish.

6

SHOW ME
THE NUMBERS

In business, if you want to understand why your company is losing money, the first thing you do is look at the expenses. I decided to take the same approach with the federal government. Almost as soon as I arrived, I could see examples of waste in something as simple as setting up my office.

Everything in Washington is defined by your status, your seniority and your party's standing, and offices are no different. Offices are assigned through seniority and a lottery system — the year you were elected and alphabetical order using your last name. More-senior members get the newer, more-desirable addresses. One of my female colleagues used her maiden name to get an earlier draw on her lottery number. Strange as it would seem in the real world, just because I was replacing John Boccieri in representing the 16th District didn't mean I'd have the same office he did. Members spend years working their way up to what they perceive as the best spots, and if a member is leaving, others have already claimed their office space. Even though my predecessor was a one-termer, he was also a "B," so he officed in the Longworth Building. As an "R," I was assigned to the 110-year-old Cannon Building. Among congressional staffers, the Cannon Building is known as Siberia. It has small, inward-facing offices more befitting a warren of rabbits than elected officials. Its offices tend to be chopped up and cluttered with file cabinets. It has too few elevators, and its fifth floor, known as "freshman row," is converted attic space where most newcomers wind up. Thanks to the way the lottery system played out, I was assigned space on Cannon's first floor, so I didn't have to deal with the elevators. Cannon is also about a six-minute walk from the Rayburn Building, which is where a lot of committee meetings are held. (The Longworth Building sits in between the other two.) I didn't mind the walk most days, and I've run my businesses out of a simple, windowless office in Wadsworth for decades. I didn't come to Washington for fancy digs; I came to work.

But there's no escaping the absurdity and expense that all this status-seeking brings. If you've ever joined a new company and been assigned an office, it probably came already furnished. That's not how it works in Washington. While the offices may change with the election cycles, the furniture in them belongs to the district. In other words, while I didn't get Boccieri's office, I did get his desk. Every time a member leaves, the House administration moves all the furniture into storage until the new representative arrives, and then they move it all to the new office. Granted, the turnover rate in the House is low. Even with the large class of freshmen in 2010, the replacement rate was only about 15 percent, and that was the highest rate in more than 50 years. But the point is that it's unnecessary to pay for moving furniture to accommodate perks of seniority that only matter inside the Beltway. My constituents didn't care where my office was or whether I had six desk drawers or only five. And most had no idea they were paying to move and store my furniture. The cost of all that moving adds up. It's ridiculous — and it's like an invisible tax to pay for the inflated egos of elected leaders.

But that's not all. Every member of Congress is given money to update their offices every five years. I have an office in Wadsworth that has served as the base for my businesses since 1983, and I'm using the same furniture today that I bought when I first opened it. But in Washington, I could change the curtains, the carpet, the chairs, my desk — whatever I wanted — every five years.

I was quickly learning that processes in Washington don't always follow a logical path. Consider what happened on my first trip home after being elected. I was used to booking my own travel, so I went online and found the cheapest airfare from Washington to Cleveland. I don't recall the exact price, but it was a good deal. Let's say it was $150. Now, of course, to get that good a deal, the ticket was nonrefundable and changing it would incur a fee. As often happens, our session didn't end on time, and I wasn't able to make the flight home at the end of the week. So, I had to rebook. Airline change fees are typically about $200, which meant I wound up spending $350 on my flight.

I turned in my receipt for reimbursement, but the House travel office refused to pay the full cost. When I complained, I was told they didn't pay for change fees, only flights. I was astounded at the absurdity. They told me I needed to book "government fare" flights. Government fares were supposedly discounted, similar to a deal that a large company might strike with an airline. But because the fares were refundable, they were more expensive than what I had paid, even with the rebooking fee. A roundtrip flight from Washington to Cleveland might be $800. Think about the absurdity: I couldn't get reimbursed for $350 because I had rebooked a nonrefundable ticket, but if I had booked an $800 ticket, the taxpayers would pick up the tab. Essentially, I was being punished for trying to save the government money. It's a small example, but it shows how waste creeps into the system.

By the way, wasteful federal travel costs aren't limited just to members' flying habits. Some actually find ways to use federal funds to get air service in their districts that the airlines wouldn't otherwise support. Johnstown, Pennsylvania, a town of less than 20,000 people, has scheduled commercial air service. From 1952 to 1990, it was represented in Congress by John Murtha, who made sure Congress allocated federal funds to subsidize flights. In other words, the government paid a commercial carrier for part of the cost of flying there to make it profitable for the airline. Across the country, the government spends hundreds of millions of dollars a year to subsidize flights to almost 160 small communities under the Essential Air Service program. Some of these are in remote areas such as Alaska or the American Southwest, where air service is, indeed, essential for deliveries of mail and medical supplies. But Johnstown is an hour and

SHOW ME THE NUMBERS

a half's drive from Pittsburgh. It's not exactly cut off from the nation's transportation grid.

Expenses like these are small potatoes in the overall scheme of federal spending, of course, but it speaks to the mindset of government and a lack of financial discipline. How can members of Congress stick to a budget if they can't see blatant examples of wasteful spending that are, literally, in front of them every day? I knew if these small expenses were out of control, larger expenses must be even more wasteful.

So, I started my quest by asking for the government's financial statement. This is not the same thing as a budget. Budgets are what you plan to spend in the future. What I wanted was an accounting of what the government had spent its money on over the previous year.

Unpacking the $4.4 trillion in government annual expenses is, of course, overwhelming. So, I decided to start with something that I thought would be simple. I told my staff to find out how much Congress spends on travel each year. I knew it would be a big number — much larger than the bill for moving and storage of office furniture. I already knew that presidents and lawmakers often flew someplace, visited a hospital or other location they could describe as an "official visit," and then attended a political event or a fundraiser, which was the primary point of the trip in the first place. The taxpayers — including the lawmakers' future opponents — paid the entire bill. Think about that: Even if you didn't vote for an elected official, you have to pay for them to travel to fundraisers so they can continue to stay in office. It's quite a system.

A big piece of the congressional travel budget is for trips to and from members' districts. Most members go back-and-forth to Washington every week. If that averages $1,000 a ticket — on "government fares," of course — and all 535 members of Congress are doing it, taxpayers are spending more than $2 million a month just to pay commuting costs for members of Congress. Lawmakers go home to fundraise and meet with constituents, but they return to Washington, in most cases, to cast votes. Much of that back-and-forth could be eliminated if members could cast votes remotely.

They would still have to come back for committee meetings, but those could be consolidated into a few weeks' time. Shortening the times when committees meet would also put more pressure on members to get things done. In the early days of the Republic, congressmen had to ride their horses, sometimes for days, to get to Washington. So, they tended to come to town, get their business done in as compressed a schedule as possible and go back to their lives. Many state legislatures still work this way. If Congress adopted similar practices, it would get more done and save the taxpayers millions of dollars a year in travel. It would also send a message to the voters: What we do in Washington is important, but it's not as important as what we do when we're home in our districts.

Travel between Washington and home districts, though, is only one piece of the travel picture. Members of Congress travel all over the world, often under the guise of trade promotion. Yet no one asks how much we are trading with that country or the purpose of that trade. There's certainly no follow-up to see if trade actually increases as a result of such a trip. Some members plan these trade "missions" years in advance to coincide with congressional recesses. If you're in Congress for 20 years, you could probably see nearly every country in the world. Not a bad perk. But it's exactly the kind of perk that we needed to review — and curtail. By the way, I never took any travel that was paid for by the federal government other than flying to and from my district.

Another reason I focused on travel was that any time I took over a business, the first thing I did was look for low-hanging fruit when it came to expenses. Normally, travel and seminars are the easiest targets. When a business is struggling and spending is out of control, the travel budget is a good place to start cutting. I was always amazed at how financially troubled companies would still be sending people all over the country, and not always for good reasons. Obviously, salespeople need to travel to clients and would-be clients because that brings in revenue. Traveling to seminars may be nice in good times, but when you're trying to cut back, it's a good place to trim. It wasn't any different for the federal government. Lots of people were flying around the world at taxpayer expense, and nobody was asking whether any of it was worth it. Some of it was, some of it wasn't. It might be necessary, for example, for members of the intelligence committee to travel to Iraq, but if a member of Ways and Means went to China to talk about trade, I thought we needed to find out what the trip cost and whether those costs justified any trade benefits we received as a result. I wanted to get a handle on what we were spending so we could start making better financial decisions.

Some travel, of course, was downright suspicious. In one case, members of the Appropriations Committee went to several countries in Africa. Why Africa? If we are not getting our appropriations passed, maybe we should stay in Washington until we do. Many of the members had their spouses with them. It was billed as a "trade mission," but how much trade are we doing with all the countries in Africa? How much did it increase from that trip? That's not to say we shouldn't try to develop trade with African nations, but at a time of trillion-dollar deficits, we should be showing more fiscal discretion, especially with travel.

My staff spent nine months trying to get complete travel expenses for the members of Congress, and they couldn't do it. We got reports from the Congressional Budget Office, and we went through them line by line. Even for a professional accountant, Washington finances can be perplexing. There's no single ledger of expenses. Sometimes expenses that are reported show up as appropriated but not authorized. Even if you can find an authorization report, then you have to find from where an item was paid. In months of digging through thousands of pages of records, my staff could never find a line item for congressional travel. It should have been easy, but it wasn't.

Since that was a dead end, I asked my staff to get the travel expenses for the president. That, too, is unavailable. It's classified. I realized we were running the government without knowing what its key expenses are. In eight years in office, I was never able to find anyone who could spell out the actual travel expenses for all elected officials. It may not be a big number in the scope of things, but when I took over a business that was losing money, only essential travel was allowed. Let's not kid ourselves, much of the congressional travel today is not essential.

🐘 🐘 🐘

My concerns about federal spending, though, were broader than a single expense item. I wanted to know how it was that Congress could so consistently spend more than it had to spend. I found my answer in the 21st Century Cures Act. Originally introduced in 2015, the bill was designed to accelerate the development of new drugs and medical devices, bringing new treatments to market more quickly. The bill allocated $6.3 billion to the National Institutes of Health and covered a wide range of medical issues. It was a great bill. But it had one notable flaw: It wasn't in the budget. The cost was spelled out, but there was no way to fund it. This was a new one to me. It's like coming home to your spouse and saying, "I bought a new car!" My wife might say: "Where's the money for that?" If I didn't have an answer, I'd be taking the car back to the dealer. Well, in Washington, not having the money for something isn't really a problem. It's more like an afterthought.

The bill was being championed by Fred Upton, a Republican from Michigan who was the chairman of the Energy and Commerce Committee at the time. That turned out to explain a lot about how this bill came to be. But first, let's remember how we think things are supposed to happen. Like many Americans, I always believed that legislation was written, discussed and amended in a committee. Perhaps hearings were held to gather more insight before drafting the legislation. Once it was drafted, other committee members could amend it. In fact, that's how things worked during my time on Financial Services under Spencer Bachus. But Bachus was the exception. The modern-day approach to legislation was quite different. Usually, the legislation was overseen by the chairman, who then shared it with his fellow party members on the committee. They might ask for tweaks that the chairman either approved or rejected. The chairman might present the bill to the full committee, but he didn't allow any amendments to it. In other words, instead of the bill being built in committee and sent up to the chairman, it was written by the chairman and sent down to the committee — or at least those members in his own party. The chairman then would move the bill to the floor — the speaker would make sure of it, assuming the chairman and the speaker got along well (which was usually the case).

Back to the committee, for a second. Why didn't ordinary members protest this clear detour of the democratic process? If you're in the same party as the chairman, you're not going to vote against the bill, because you won't remain on the committee for long if you do. It's not uncommon for committee chairs to ask incoming members if they "stand with the committee." So, as a practical matter, committee members can't vote "no." The only people on a committee who can vote against the chairman without recourse are the people who wouldn't ordinarily vote with the chairman anyway — members of the minority party. As a result, support for most bills coming out of committee is split along party lines.

In the case of the Cures Act, it received some Democratic support as well, because, as I said, it was a good bill. But it was also a budget buster. By the time it hit the House floor, we had already passed our budget, and the money for the Cures Act wasn't in it. In Washington, not having the money is not a problem. If you want to pass a bill that the government can't afford, you simply go — ironically — to the Rules Committee.

The Rules Committee is one of the most misnamed entities in Washington because it exists, in fact, to bypass the rules. It's made up of a special group, appointed by the speaker and the minority leader, at whose pleasure the members serve. It functions as an interim place that bills go through after they come out of committee and before they hit the House floor. Its original purpose was to ensure that no bills reached the floor without complying with the rules of the House. But over the years, it has twisted that power into the authority to pass the bill on for a floor vote even if there's no money for it. Essentially, the committee can waive the budget.

The Rules Committee could waive other rules, too. For example, House rules say that a bill must be made public three days before it's voted on. But the committee can, and frequently does, waive that requirement. That's how we end up with votes on bills that no one has read.

The Rules Committee is, fundamentally, a political body. It recognizes political realities and acts to make it possible for the House to meet those realities. Again, this isn't how most rules work. If I want to do something in my city but it's against the rules, there isn't a city committee set up to bend the rules on my behalf for that one day. But in Congress, the rules of ordinary life are often suspended. And in the case of the Cures Act, the rules were getting in the way of what Congress wanted to do. The act was, indeed, popular. It was touted as a medical necessity, and since it was about funding cancer research, it was about as popular as apple pie. Both Democrats and Republicans lined up to pass it. When the Republican whips — the people who rally supporters of a given bill — came to me, I refused to vote for it because it didn't meet the budget. As I saw it, we had a process and we broke that process. We can't make exceptions for every piece of legislation that someone deems important. After all, most legislation is important to somebody. The process, the regular order of the way things are supposed to work, is designed to put a priority on legislation. The Cures Act was a good bill, but it never should have gotten to the floor because it skirted the funding requirements. We can't simply break the rules because we find it expedient in the moment.

Earlier I said that no one in Washington can follow a budget, and this is why. They've created an institutional process that ensures they don't have to. The rules are meant to be waived and broken.

The Upton version of the bill in 2015, by the way, passed the House but not the Senate. A revised bill in 2016 passed both chambers and was signed into law by President Obama. The difference was the second bill had "paid-fors" in it. Paid-fors are a financial rationalization for how a bill will be funded. They stipulate that some cuts will be made elsewhere to fund new spending. But like the Rules Committee, paid-fors are often bogus. They're budget gimmicks that present a veneer of fiscal responsibility. One of my favorites is when Congress delays sending out checks by a day so that the dollars come out of one year's budget and not the other's. It's the same money, and it's the same unfunded deficit, it just gets assigned to a different fiscal year. Only in Washington can this be considered paying for something. Everywhere else in America, such accounting chicanery is laughed at. In certain corporations, it might get you thrown in jail.

I saw this firsthand in 2015, when I was on the Budget Committee and we passed a federal highway spending bill. I voted against the bill even though it had been combined with another bill that I had worked on, got sponsors for and that would save the Treasury money. My bill was inserted into the larger one to help get my vote, but I still voted no. My colleagues couldn't believe I would vote against my own bill, but the problem was that the highway funding bill had paid-fors that assumed, for instance, we could sell oil from the Strategic Petroleum Reserve at $83 a barrel. The price of oil had been falling for months. In fact, oil barely cracked $60 that year, and by December 2015, it had fallen to almost $37. Everyone knew that the government wasn't going to sell oil for anything close to $83, but that assumption and several others gave lawmakers the cover or the paid-fors we needed for the highway bill. So, of course, the bill led to more debt. I could see that coming, and that's why I voted against it.

Unfortunately, the way the system works now, there's absolutely no effort to impose discipline on it. My vote against the bill was no different than standing in the middle of Times Square with a giant sign that says: "Repent, the End Is Near." Nobody paid much attention to my protest because, in the end, the leadership controls everything. They decide whether to bring a bill to the floor or let it die in committee, and they decide to wash the bills they want through the Rules Committee, so they don't have to be paid for. By the way, the Rules Committee is composed of seven members of the majority and only four members of the minority, so the majority pretty much wins every vote because, again, no one in the majority is going to vote against the leadership's wishes.

To make this problem worse, Congress budgets for 10 years, but it does it every year. So, no matter what you do, you can push it off for 10 years. This perpetual 10-year window comes courtesy of the Congressional Budget Office. The CBO was created as part of the budget reconciliation measures adopted in 1974, and part of its job is to assess the financial impact of legislation on the budget.

CBO staffers examine the detail of each bill and generate a financial assessment, based on a 10-year projection. The problem is that Congress takes these assessments at face value, and no one goes back and looks ten years later to see if the assessment was accurate. So, the CBO keeps doing things the same way it's always done them.

Unfortunately, a ten-year window simply isn't long enough. Congress can easily kick a can down the road for ten years and hide the high costs of a bill in the next decade. In fact, lawmakers have become adept at throwing the garbage eleven or twelve years down the road. That's what happened with the Affordable Care Act. The ACA was passed and based on a budgetary and spending standpoint of the first ten years. What do you think happens in the eleventh, twelfth and thirteenth years? Everything blows up. We're in the eleventh year now, and that's why you're starting to see expenses skyrocket.

During my time on the Budget Committee, we held hearings on improving the budget process for two years while Rep. Tom Price was still committee chair. (He later served as secretary of Health and Human Services before resigning in 2017 after being accused of running up $400,000 in unauthorized flights on chartered planes.) One proposal we looked at would have required anyone sponsoring a bill that broke the budget to present it on the House floor, explain its budget impact, and justify the expense. That would have been fun to watch — or at least I thought so at the time. Another idea, which I pushed for, was to have Congress present an annual financial statement comparing actual government spending with the budget. As soon as Price left the committee to work in the administration, those efforts stopped.

That's how it worked, sadly. Those of us who cared about these issues might get some momentum, and with the right committee chair, we would have someone to champion our ideas. But once those committee chairs flipped roles it was difficult to make headway on long-term problems. And our happy band of brothers on the Budget Committee was especially hard-hit by this because so few people wanted to even be there. Most members did everything they could to get off of it as quickly as possible. I'm not sure what they were worried about, because no matter how they voted to cut spending, there was no follow-through. Spending just kept rising.

But, in the end, politics gave me my answer. Every time you took a vote to cut spending, it was like paying for a political ad against yourself in the future. Every government program has a constituency, and in the hands of a half-decent political operative, any voter can be convinced that a spending cut was going to imperil life, liberty and the pursuit of justice. That bridge to nowhere? You could argue it played a vital role connecting rural Alaskans to medical care and educational opportunities. A $1,000 air ticket to get from Washington to Cleveland? That could be spun as a way for voters to make their voices heard. No wonder I lost the battle — and the war — on the Cures Act. Nobody makes a long political career out of votes opposing cancer research. Later, my political opponents accused me of voting to cut Medicare, for example. Well, I didn't. I voted to cut spending across the board so that we could balance the budget. I didn't target Medicare but good luck explaining that in thirty seconds or less. The fact is that if you truly believe in cutting spending, you'll have someone fighting you all the way and nobody in your corner. It's about the loneliest fight in Washington.

Deficits did go down during my tenure, but it wasn't because we were able to instill financial discipline. We cut the deficit the Washington way — we waited until we were forced to. And then even when it happened, we went screaming and crying to do what we should have been doing all along.

In 2013, we implemented automatic spending cuts through a process known as sequestration that was included in the Budget

Control Act of 2011. Basically, because we couldn't balance the budget, we were required ourselves to cut discretionary social programs and defense spending across the board. It wasn't strategic or targeted, but it got the job done. So, we cut about $1 trillion out of the deficit in seven years, but most of that was because of sequestration, and about 80 percent of those cuts came from the military budget. Major expenses like entitlement programs and veterans' benefits weren't included. It may look like we cut the deficit, but we didn't do it willingly. I was able to say I left Congress while the deficits were coming down, but it was a false premise. And naturally, it wouldn't last.

7

FISCAL STATE OF THE UNION

In business, knowing what happened in the past helps you to make better financial decisions in the future. You probably do much the same thing with your own bank account. You may look over your spending each month and see where your money went. It helps you make decisions such as cutting back on eating out or other expenses. But the federal government has no rearview mirror when it comes to its finances.

I must admit to being surprised that not only did the federal government not have a financial statement, nobody seemed interested in creating one. I still run six companies, and on my desk as I write this are several two-inch thick binders with financial statements for the previous year for several of them. I can flip open one of the books and see exactly how much that business sold, what its profits were and what it spent money on.

I realized part of the problem was that the government couldn't create a financial statement because it didn't have any standards to base it on. Private businesses, especially those that are publicly traded, use guidelines from the Financial Accounting Standards Board, or FASB. These Generally Accepted Accounting Principles, as they're known, are a uniform set of reporting standards, so that investors are looking at the same information no matter what the company is. (Some companies prefer to use other standards, but they still also must report their finances under GAAP.)

I knew that there were also standards set down by the Government Accounting Standards Board that were designed to reflect the special accounting needs of governments. GASB standards, it turns out, are used at the state and local levels, but the federal government doesn't follow those, either.

When I asked why, I was told, as I often was in Washington, that I simply didn't understand. The federal government, the line goes, faces different conditions than other public entities or governing bodies. That's true, in a sense: The federal government owns assets that are difficult to value, such as federal park land or naval destroyers in the middle of the ocean. We have things like the Social Security system. It's definitely a liability, but how you account for it depends on whether you spread out its costs over sixty-five, seventy-five, or more years.

But as difficult as these issues are, they aren't insurmountable. As a CPA, I know a few things about putting together financial statements. Sure, some assets and liabilities are hard to value. You basically make the best estimate you can, you add a footnote explaining how you came to that value, and then you adjust it in the future if those values change. Companies do this all the time. They assign values to rocket ships, the estimated value of oil and minerals in the ground, and the public's perception of their products or brands. Surely, we could come up with a value for a battleship and, yes, even the Grand Canyon. It might actually make it a lot easier to spend on our Park Service if we knew how valuable those parks are! As for Social Security and its liabilities, that's easy. Just pick the length of time of the liability. This is exactly what GASB does for state and local governments that must account for public pension liabilities.

As it happens, if you ask enough questions and challenge people's assumptions, you find other people who share your concerns. In fact, there was a group, the Federal Accounting Standards Advisory Board, that was supposed to create the very standards I sought. It was formed in 1990 to improve federal financial reporting, but even though it had been around for thirty years, it hadn't actually set the standards necessary to compile a financial statement. The more I tried to get answers, the more I got the runaround. I also met resistance from people who you'd think would want the government to set and uphold higher standards, including the American Institute of Certified Public Accountants, which, it turns out, didn't want the government involved in setting accounting standards of any kind.

My quest for a financial statement ultimately led me to the Government Accountability Office (formerly the General Accounting Office). The GAO staffers I met with brushed me off just like everyone else had. The agency had been around for a hundred years, and they didn't need some upstart congressman telling them how to do their jobs.

I did finally get the Congressional Budget Office to send me a 700-page document that it claimed could serve as a financial statement. It wasn't an accounting. It was just a collection of financial gobbledygook that no CPA would be able to decipher meaningfully. There was no summary. It was just a bunch of numbers and data strewn together. The more I looked, and the more resistance I encountered, the more it became clear that the problem wasn't that no one in government knew what anything cost. The problem was that no one in government wanted to know what anything cost.

🐘 🐘 🐘

While my inquiries may have been fruitless, they didn't go unnoticed. One day in 2015, one of my staffers told me that Gene Dodaro, the comptroller general, wanted to talk to me. The comptroller general is a position many people don't even know exists. Basically, he runs the GAO, but in recent years, the job has morphed into being the nation's primary fiscal scold, warning anybody who will listen about the impending crisis because of the federal budget deficit. Dodaro, who was appointed by President Obama, wasn't the first person who held that job to beat the drum about the government's financial mismanagement. His predecessor, David Walker, a George W. Bush appointee, did the same thing. In fact, Walker used to produce an annual report that was similar to what I was looking for. Every year he would hold a press conference to announce the report's release. Hardly anyone showed up. Other government agencies dismissed his annual report as irrelevant. Walker eventually quit and went to work for Pete Peterson, a billionaire who had set up a foundation focused on fixing America's debt problem.

Dodaro took over and carried on Walker's tradition of trying to get people in Washington to care about the deficit. He told me that he had come to the conclusion that the reason nothing changed in Congress was because no one in government wanted to be reminded of the country's perilous financial condition. But instead of fighting the inertia and apathy from his office in Washington, he decided to take the show on the road, and had been going around the country and discussing the government's financial position with any group, newspaper board or anyone else who would listen. I asked him who he had talked to, and he rattled off some names.

"Have you talked to the president?" I asked.

"Yes," he said.

"Is he listening?"

"No."

That, of course, was a big part of the problem. No one in a position of leadership wanted to hear an honest accounting of the nation's debt-ridden books, nor come to grips with the financial crisis all that debt would create. There are lots of reasons why $22 trillion in debt is bad, of course, but for me, one of the most important is the implications it has for national security. As the debt grows, so does our interest expense on that debt. A 1 percent increase in interest rates today amounts to about $2 trillion in additional debt over ten years. That's simply unsustainable. At a time when we are already struggling to figure out how to meet the future liabilities of Social Security, Medicare and Medicaid, a rising national debt is a prelude to crisis.

It has sometimes been necessary for us to increase our national debt in times of national hardship, such as World War II or even the implosion of the housing market in 2008. But now, we're growing our debt during times of prosperity. This is precisely the time we should be paying down the debt. Keep in mind that during World War II, we grew the debt to almost the same size as the economy, but in the boom years that followed, we paid it down. Today, we have a booming economy and a ballooning debt.

That money is borrowed from someone and, increasingly, that someone is China. China is the largest foreign owner of our debt, holding about $1.2 trillion worth of Treasuries. We are literally mortgaging our future to a country that doesn't particularly like us, and that is becoming the biggest economic and military power in Asia.

By the way, China is the biggest foreign debt holder, but the biggest holder of the national debt, by far, is you. The Social Security Trust Fund holds about 48 percent of the debt, retirement funds for federal employees hold another 22 percent, and military retirement funds hold 14 percent. Medicare holds another 5 percent. So the debt concerns hit closer to home than you might think.

Dodaro actually had a lot of the answers I was looking for. He sat right across my desk and told me bluntly that the country was headed for a financial catastrophe. If we didn't change our borrow-and-spend habits, the deficit was destined to grow at such a rapid pace that in twenty years, the United States would be in a situation similar to the one Greece faced in 2009.

For those who don't remember or didn't pay attention at the time, the European Union saved Greece from economic collapse in what became the biggest rescue of a bankrupt country ever. By 2009, Greece's budget deficit exceeded its total economic output, and due to less-than-stellar tax compliance, there was little confidence that Greece could tax its way back to fiscal health. That triggered a market sell-off of the country's bonds, which basically were claims on future tax revenues, and meant that current and future financial needs couldn't be met at anywhere near affordable prices. It was like someone who is unemployed trying to borrow more money to pay their living expenses, and every bank in town turning them down, except that person was an entire country. Unable to finance its needs, Greece turned to the EU for help. Various European authorities pumped almost 320 billion euros (or about $360 billion — enough to cover about a quarter of America's debt to China) into Greece to keep it afloat. The trade-off was that the bailout package required the country to adopt severe austerity measures — cuts in government services and transfer payments — as a provision of the loans. While the austerity program strengthened the government's finances, it also triggered a deep recession. Greece will be paying off that debt until at least 2060.

There would be no EU to bail out the U.S. if we wound up in similar straits. Few countries could afford the support we would need. China might be able to, but the idea of being at the mercy of China is unsettling to say the least. Because China is one of the biggest holders of the debt we've already issued, by the time we reached the need for a bailout, we might have dragged China down with us — or it would already have so much leverage over us that it wouldn't provide additional help.

As a percentage of our GDP, our deficit remains well below that of Greece — about 3.8 percent in fiscal 2018 — but the deficit is only part of the picture. Each year we run a deficit, which is the gap between what the government spends and the revenue it collects, it adds to the national debt, which is the total amount the government owes. In February 2019, the debt topped a record $22 trillion. We've added a trillion dollars to the debt just in the past year. It's easy to not worry about this, of course. The economy is strong, unemployment is low, the stock market is rising, and, let's face it, nobody really knows what a trillion dollars looks like anyway. But the debt and deficit are perpetual thunderheads on our financial horizon.

Dodaro argues that if we keep racking up deficits, and we keep piling on debt, investors will lose confidence in our ability to pay, and that will mean that they will stop buying up Treasuries as if they're the safest investment around. If that happens, we will hit a wall. We will be unable to finance government operations and then the government will not just shut down but also begin to break down, because there will be no money to pay for vital programs. It won't matter if the spending is discretionary or not. Everything from Social Security checks to military programs could be at risk.

As Dodaro was explaining all this, a bell went off in my head.

"Can I get you to deliver a Fiscal State of the Union address?" I asked. As I understood the rules of the House, the speaker could invite basically anyone to address the chamber and that included the comptroller general. Why not have Dodaro come before Congress and give an annual update of our overall financial position, just like the president does in the State of the Union address?

I decided to put a resolution together to prod John Boehner into making the request. I took the idea to my bipartisan breakfast group. After a little persuasion, I got all of them — thirteen Republicans and thirteen Democrats — to co-sponsor a bill calling for the comptroller general to make an annual Fiscal State of the Union address to a joint session of the House and the Senate. It was such a commonsense bill. In business, every year your chief financial officer makes an annual report to the board about the financial health of the company. All I wanted was for the comptroller general to do the same thing for the federal government.

Eventually, we got almost 200 co-sponsors from both parties to sign on. We needed 218 and the blessing of the party leadership to send the bill to the floor. You could have 300 sponsors and if the leadership blocked it, it wasn't going anywhere.

That's where I ran into trouble. I asked Kevin McCarthy, who was the Republican majority leader, if we could move the bill forward.

"Are you crazy?" he asked. "You want the comptroller general to say where we're at with our finances?"

I told him I did.

"That," he said, "will cause nothing but calamity. That cannot happen."

He suggested that instead we hold a hearing in front of the Financial Services Committee, which at the time was run by Jeb Hensarling of Texas. I went to Hensarling, explained my idea and asked if we could put the Fiscal State of the Union on the agenda for his committee. I pointed out that I had 200 sponsors.

Once again, I was told I couldn't do that. I asked why.

"You'll cause the bond markets to collapse," he said.

"What are you talking about?" I asked.

"If you start having somebody talk about our fiscal state, the bond market will just collapse."

I told him I had a hard time believing that. He told me that if we honestly disclosed the country's financial state, bond rating agencies like Moody's Investors Service and Standard & Poor's would cut our ratings, and the resulting sell-off of Treasury bonds would cause the market to implode.

I left the meeting thinking maybe Hensarling had a point. I didn't agree, but he always seemed like a thoughtful guy. So, I set up a meeting with the president of Moody's. When I arrived in his office in lower Manhattan, I got right to the point: Would the bond market collapse if we disclosed the financial state of the country in a public address?

He laughed.

"You don't think we know what the financial state of the country is? I have sixty-five people in this office who do nothing but work on an annual statement about the finances of the federal government, and based on that analysis we issue ratings on the government's debt every year. We know exactly where you're at."

I asked if I could see the statement. He told me I couldn't because it was proprietary. He said the bottom line was that the rating could fall if something changed that affected the country's finances — not because we, as government officials, decided to discuss the situation honestly. (In fact, in 2011, S&P lowered the U.S. bond rating for the first time in history.)

I went back to Washington armed with the information that the truth would not destroy the market for U.S. Treasuries, but I still couldn't get any traction for my bill. I was surprised at members of both parties who told me they didn't want the American people to know the true state of the government's finances. I remember one in particular — Brad Sherman, a Democrat from California — because he was a CPA like me. He said: "Do you think I want people in my district to see what the numbers are down here?"

The bill wound up dying without reaching the House floor, but I kept bringing it up before the Budget Committee. The debate continued, and some of the strongest opposition came from my Republican colleagues. At one point, someone even suggested that rather than having a speech, we should just boil the finances down to a simple statement that fit on a postcard and then mail it to the American people. I argued people would just throw it away because there wouldn't be enough information there for anyone to really understand it. Besides, I knew that Congress needed to see it even more than the American people. That's why you needed to have someone who knows what they're doing walk them through the finances step by step and explain the severity of the situation. More important, we also needed to explain the consequences of inaction.

I did finally get the Budget Committee to invite Dodaro for a hearing, but most of the members didn't even bother to show up.

After he presented the bleak outlook for the country's finances, one of the other committee members asked: "So when is the problem going to occur?"

"It's up to you," Dodaro replied. "It's going to be in the next twenty years. It could be sooner. It just depends on what you all do."

I realized the committee member asking the question wasn't concerned with fixing the problem; he wanted to make sure he'd be out of office before the problem became a crisis. No one in Congress, it seemed, wanted to know about, let alone discuss, the long-term financial health of the country they were supposed to be governing.

Although the committee never invited Dodaro back again, I got a call in late 2018 from Kathleen Rice, a Democrat from New York, who asked if she could pick up where we left off and resume the call for a Fiscal State of the Union. So now the Democrats are driving the idea. I'm glad someone was willing to take up the cause, but I don't believe Rice will find members of her own party any more willing to address the issue than I did. There are just too many reasons why members of Congress would be embarrassed by the public airing of that information. After all, they're responsible for most of it.

🐷 🐷 🐷

At one of my last budget hearings before I left office, the director of the Congressional Budget Office testified before the committee. It quickly devolved into the same old thing: Republicans attacking Democrats and Democrats attacking Republicans. Nobody was listening to the witness, who was providing financial projections for the next decade. The CBO said it expected federal revenue to increase by 60 percent in ten years.

When it came my turn to speak, I said, "If you were the controller at my company and you came to me and told me that our revenues were going to grow by 60 percent over the next ten years, I'd slap you on the back and say, 'Let's go get a beer.' The problem, though, is there's something else in this report. It says expenses are going to grow by 85 percent over the next ten years. The trend lines are horrible. You're telling me that we have this great revenue growth — that we're going to bring more into the Treasury than in any year in our history, but you're also telling me that we're heading for trouble."

He agreed with my assessment, and I asked him to tell me what was causing these trends.

"Demographics," he said.

I was a little surprised he answered so directly, but I appreciated his candor. Next, I asked him to explain what he meant.

"Medicare, Medicaid and Social Security," he said. "The programs continue to grow."

And then he added: "But it can be fixed."

I asked him how.

"Well, look," he said. "The projections are not good. There's revenue things you could fix; there's expense things you could fix." And he began to go through some of those possibilities.

Finally, I stopped him, because I only had five minutes, and I said, "OK, so let's say we increase Social Security payroll taxes by 100 percent. Will that fix the problem?"

He said it wouldn't.

My time ran out, and a Democrat took his turn and asked if we could solve the problem by raising income taxes. The CBO director said in theory we could. Then the Democrat pointed at the Republicans on the committee and said, "They don't want to raise taxes; they just did a tax cut," and once again the discussion spiraled down into political carping. That's why I kept pushing for a financial statement. Because it's a document that lays out the hard facts, without the political commentary. It can't be shouted down or talked over or have its time taken away. It would be an irrefutable statement of the trouble the country faces, and that's exactly why so many of my colleagues in Congress worked to make sure it didn't happen.

🐘 🐘 🐘

You'd think that given the problems Congress has been willing to take on — fighting wars, regulating Wall Street, paying for people's health care and retirement, and so on — it would be willing to take on the problem of deficits. But deficits don't get solved easily, and politicians hate problems without easy answers. Every year, it simply becomes more difficult for the government to live within its means, and it's far easier to just throw a little more debt on the pile and act as if there's nothing to worry about.

As I mentioned, 85 percent of the budget is essentially untouchable, especially Medicare, Medicaid and Social Security. Entitlements already constitute more than 70 percent of federal spending, but the scary thing is that it's increased from where it was just twenty years ago — 43 percent of the budget. Cutting these programs — even appearing to rein them in — can be political suicide. I mentioned that when I ran for the Senate in 2018, my opponent accused me of wanting to cut Medicare just because in the Budget Committee I raised the issue of trying to slow its growth so it could be sustained. But if you say you want to touch Medicare and Social Security, your political opponent will go straight to senior voters — and they vote.

So, the most politically expedient strategy is to have no strategy. When the federal debt hit $22 trillion in February 2019, there were a few obligatory news stories about it, and then it went away. Nobody in Washington was talking about it. Talking about it isn't going to help in the next election cycle. The average member of the House serves for seven years, and the average senator serves for eleven. Most of them do the math and just decide to wait out the issue. But many Senators and members of Congress stay far longer, and still, they do nothing. Republican Senate Majority Leader Mitch McConnell's been in office thirty-five years and he's done nothing to address the problem. What's his excuse?

The fundamental problem with these programs is that all the numbers are working against them. For example, when Medicare was created in 1965, the average life expectancy was sixty-seven years for men and it was seventy-five for women. Today, it's seventy-six years for men and eighty-one for women. That's great news, but it means that people are on these programs for far longer than we anticipated when they were launched. And contrary to what you may think, Medicare and Social Security taxes do not go into some kind of account, to be saved for when the government needs the money for you. They are pay-as-you-go plans — today's workers pay for today's retirees at today's dollars. The average couple contributes about $134,000 to Medicare during their working life, and they withdraw an average of $330,000 in benefits. For today's seniors, it's a great deal. You put in a dollar and you get three back. But it's unsustainable, especially if we have fewer workers for each retiree, which is exactly the case. We now have 10,000 people a day retiring, and the growth in the number of retirees is far exceeding the growth in our workforce. And, oh, by the way, health care is far more expensive than it used to be. When Medicare was initially passed into law, we didn't have joint replacements, heart stents and advanced biologic medicine — all of which are accessible for today's seniors. Again, these medical miracles are wonderful because they're keeping us alive and active longer, but we need to admit that they're expensive to provide.

In mid-2018, *The New York Times* reported that the Medicare trust fund will be depleted in 2026. What was significant about the story was that it noted that just one year earlier, in 2017, the government had predicted the fund would run out of money in 2029. In one year, we cut three years from the lifespan of Medicare. So the end is coming pretty fast if we do nothing.

By the way, private industry has already recognized and addressed this problem.

Corporations used to offer gold-plated pensions to their workers. They figured they could afford them, and it would improve long-term loyalty. You'll notice that few of them still have pensions today. The numbers were simply unsustainable. Operations like manufacturing became more efficient, requiring fewer workers, and suddenly the ranks of the retired far outnumbered those currently on the payroll. Overseas competitors got better and took away some business, further cutting into jobs. Instead of nine employees paying for one retiree, they found themselves with one employee paying for three retirees. The same thing is happening with the federal government's social entitlements. The system is upside down — too many people are taking out, and not enough are putting in.

When I was growing up, my parents, despite all their financial struggles, thought of Social Security as supplemental retirement income, and they saved on their own as a result. Today, Social Security has become essential for many people, which only makes fixing the problem more difficult. The longer we wait, the harder it gets.

The solutions to these problems are painful. We don't need to eliminate entitlements, but we must fix them in one of two ways: Adjust benefits down or increase revenue to pay for the benefits we provide now. Adjusting benefits could come in a number of ways. For example, we could raise the age at which people receive them. But that upends the plans of those who are close to retirement. Understandably, if we push off the retirement age for today's fifty-something workers, they'll feel they've lost something they were promised.

But there are other ways we can adjust benefits: by raising the payroll taxes that pay for Social Security. Currently, Social Security taxes are capped. Nobody pays more than $7,960.80 a year in Social Security taxes (Medicare taxes, by comparison, are uncapped). You pay Social Security tax only on income up to $132,900 a year. We can raise those caps, and we have, but again it's not something members of Congress want to draw attention to — even though it would help solve the problem. We also could adopt a means test, the results of which would identify people whose net worth was above a certain level and who would not receive benefits — or they'd see far lower benefits than everyone else. That will anger those who paid into the system with the intent of getting something back, and it might undermine the popularity of the program. But it would have one clear-cut benefit: It would essentially turn Social Security into insurance against having no income in your post-working years. Not everyone saves for their own retirement, and Social Security should be there for them; but for people who earn more and can save more, the benefit won't be as necessary, and so we should provide less of it — or even none of it — to them.

Obviously, all of these are hard choices, but if we're going to fix Social Security so that it's there for the people who need it most, it's going to require adopting new policies.

Raising revenue would require addressing another problem that is as politically divisive as the idea of cutting the programs: immigration. Again, it comes down to simple math. Americans aren't having as many children as they once did. We used to have an average of about 3.4 children per household. Back then, we didn't need our immigration system to be as vibrant, because we were making our own workforce inside our country. Today, Americans have an average of 1.5 children per household, so there're fewer potential workers. And the population is aging rapidly. The only reasonable solution is an immigration system that allows for people with needed skills to come here, get educated and stay — and pay taxes into the system as well. Hospitals, hotels, construction companies, dairy farmers, meat packers, vegetable growers and numerous other industries have a huge need for labor. But with the caps on immigration, and the fact that most native-born children don't grow up wanting to do work in the fields or clean hotel rooms, we simply aren't meeting that demand.

If we're going to maintain economic growth and develop a base to keep funding entitlements, we need a system that brings in more workers and allows them to legally participate in programs such as Social Security and Medicare. Ideas that would help get us there come and go, but rarely do they go anywhere. Our broken immigration system has been largely unchanged since the 1990s, and no one in Congress can agree on even the most basic steps for fixing it — not better paths to citizenship, not better approaches to worker visas (including better enforcement), not more seasonal worker programs. They'd prefer to hammer the other side, using immigration as a cudgel. Democrats paint Republicans as xenophobic; Republicans paint Democrats as uninterested in border security. They're both wrong. But both sides have a convenient excuse for not doing something that could actually solve a problem that all of America should be screaming about. It's like they have a handshake agreement to create as much hysteria as possible over fake problems so that nobody ever notices the real problems. And it's working.

8

MAKING CRISES

It's easy to complain about Congress' runaway spending or say we need to do something about the deficit. But when you look at *how* Congress spends money, the full scale of the problem comes into view. There's little long-term thinking or appreciation for the future economic impact of what Congress spends or whether the spending actually solves the problem it was supposed to address. As a result, much of the money Congress spends today is to fix problems it created in years past. Then Congress takes credit for fixing the problem, without acknowledging that they or their predecessors caused it in the first place.

The starkest example, of course, is the situation in Iraq and Syria. We invaded Iraq, removed a dictator, spent trillions trying to stabilize and rebuild the country, only to create a power vacuum that led to a more-protracted conflict, and then the creation of the Islamic State terror organization. We thought we were doing the right thing, but in the end, we made an even bigger problem, and we spent even more money trying to fix it.

As expensive and dramatic as it was, it's just one example. There are thousands of others. Congress frequently tries to solve one problem, creates several others, then tries to solve those, creating even more problems. It's like a giant game of whack-a-mole, except each time you play, it costs the taxpayers a few billion dollars.

The Iraq War and resulting battle to restore order was one example, but that was far from home. Here's one that people felt in their backyards: the opioid epidemic. Opioids are medications that reduce the intensity of pain signatures sent to the brain. They've been used for centuries to treat acute pain, but beginning in the 1990s, they were increasingly prescribed for chronic pain or even situations in which people were recovering from surgery but didn't need such powerful medications. Over the ensuing two decades, as opioids became more widely distributed, and people began taking them on a longer-term basis, it also became clear that they were highly addictive. People who were prone to addiction increasingly sought out opioids, not for pain relief, but to provide a high. The drugs were increasingly diverted onto the black market, so instead of going to patients who needed them, they went to people who didn't. Tens of thousands of Americans were using opioids no differently than, say, crack cocaine or other potent narcotics. But instead of coming from distant countries via vast networks of illegal drugs, opioids were coming from American labs and American pharmacies.

Overdose rates began rising. More than 47,000 Americans died of opioid overdoses in 2017, and 1.7 million people suffered from substance abuse issues related to opioids, according to the National Institute on Drug Abuse.

Clearly this was a national crisis, but how did it happen? And what, if anything, could Congress do to fix it? I knew that to really understand the problem, I needed to hear from people who were directly involved, not just people who thought they were experts. Back home in Ohio, which had an explosion of opioid abuse, I formed what I called my opioid panel, which was made up of medical experts and operators of recovery centers, as well as parents who had lost children to opioid overdoses and several recovering addicts.

It's unusual to have recovering drug addicts on a congressional fact-finding panel, but I felt it was important to understand, firsthand, what drove their addiction. One of the first things they talked about surprised me. It had nothing to do with the easy availability of painkillers or doctors prescribing too many of them. It had to do with education.

Let me explain. In the past few decades, we changed our educational system to focus on sending all kids to college. Not only did most parents, including Tina and myself, want their kids to go to college, but also many lawmakers believed a college education should be encouraged. The government expanded programs for low-interest loans, Pell Grants and other forms of federally subsidized financial aid. Politicians believed they were supporting educational opportunities for everyone, and more important, removing the financial barriers to a college education. When I was growing up, the main reason someone didn't go to college was because they couldn't afford it. Those who didn't go to college could get a job in the steel mill or the coal mine, and while it was hard work, they could still earn a good middle-class living.

But the gap between people who earned only a high school degree and those with a college degree started widening in the 1970s, as America's manufacturing industries pulled back. And so, as a nation, we began to push more kids into college track classes. While that may have been an admirable idea, the focus on college preparation in high schools largely eliminated vocational programs. The former addicts on my panel said they felt the system — the school system and, indirectly, the political system — was telling them they had no value if they didn't pass their college-prep classes. But what happens to those students who didn't want to take trigonometry or couldn't pass it no matter how hard they tried? Thirty years ago, that same kid might have excelled at welding or electrical wiring, but today he found himself passed over by a system in which politicians had decided that the only path to success was through college.

One of the former addicts on my panel said, "I didn't want to take those classes, and they told me I would be useless." He stopped trying and wound up hanging out with his friends and raiding his parents' medicine cabinet before they came home from work. And there they found a bottle of opioids.

How did that bottle get there? Once again, it was a government policy. Politicians decided that treatment under federally funded programs like Medicare and Medicaid should ensure that patients are pain-free. Doctors and other medical providers were graded on whether they had eliminated pain on behalf of their patients —

not just acute pain from surgery but also chronic pain from more ordinary sources. Think about the difference between the pain you feel from surgery and the pain you feel from a chronic bad back. They're both painful, but if doctors are trying to eliminate pain in any form, they will prescribe the strongest medicine to the problem — opioids — especially if they are getting paid to do so or criticized for the quality of pain care if they don't. And Medicare began to pay for it. Many patients found opioids provided more effective relief than traditional painkillers such as aspirin and ibuprofen. Some people struggle with severe chronic pain, and I understand their desire to seek medication that will give them relief. In many cases, traditional painkillers just don't work. But the widespread availability of opioids also meant that doctors prescribed them in cases where, in the past, people would have taken less-addictive medications, or done physical therapy to ease the pain. When I was in high school, I was in a serious motorcycle accident. I will never forget heading to the hospital in the back of the ambulance. The driver called in to the hospital on the radio as I was being transferred, "We have a motorcycle accident, possible broken back, broken arm, broken leg and internal injuries." Fortunately, nothing was broken, and I had no internal injuries, but I bit through my tongue and had some pretty severe bruises and cuts. My mother was a nurse, and she basically handed me a bottle of aspirin and sent me to school the next day. I was in pain, but it didn't preclude me from going to class. Today, the doctor might have shown me a chart with smiley faces and asked me to rate my pain, prescribed me a pill bottle full of opioids and told me to stay home for three weeks.

The point is that changing expectations by doctors and patients about pain management contributed to the wider use of opioids. And there was one final bureaucratic requirement that came into play: under Medicare, prescriptions must be good for sixty days to qualify for reimbursement.

As a result, doctors prescribed larger doses — bigger bottles — which resulted in more pills in more medicine cabinets. Granted, many doctors wrote the prescriptions because they believed, based on what drug manufacturers told them, that opioids were safe and nonaddictive. But the entire issue would have been moot if the federal programs had not inadvertently created a surge in supply.

Today, many state attorneys general are suing the drug companies for making and marketing opioids. This is ridiculous. The drug companies simply provided something that everyone wanted. If you're going to sue them, you also have to sue the physicians, the distributors and even the politicians, because after all, they ordered that opioids be covered by insurance and distributed widely.

It's worth noting that it isn't just young people who are getting addicted. We're seeing more and more elderly also getting hooked on opioids. Even someone who's taking them for legitimate reasons can get hooked if they have a 60-day supply. The situation has become a national crisis, and in late 2018, President Trump secured $6 billion in federal funds to fight the problem over the next two years. You know you have a costly mistake on your hands if it takes $6 billion to fix it. But again, that $6 billion is going to fix a problem that the federal government and politicians helped create. Not only do taxpayers pay for it, but they also often suffer the consequences.

👾 👾 👾

I mentioned that some of the recovering addicts on my opioid panel cited the pressure to go to college as one factor that drove their addiction and that the government has encouraged a college-for-all attitude by funding low-interest educational loans. Opioid addiction aside, higher education is another government-backed crisis waiting to happen.

I juggled multiple jobs putting myself through school, and, yes, I relied on some student loans for help. But in those days, student loans could be used only for tuition and books. Now, they're much easier to get, and they can be used for almost anything while you're in school. The expansion of federal grants and loans for education has spawned a cottage industry in the private sector as well. Almost anyone can borrow tens of thousands of dollars — often at double-digit interest rates — under the guise of furthering their education.

I hear stories about students taking on huge amounts of debt and using loans for things that have nothing to do with college, like cars or even breast implants. I met an engineering student in Youngstown, Ohio, who had an idea for a new product, but he needed $60,000 to develop it. He already had an interested buyer who was willing to pay him $75,000, but he couldn't get a loan for his development costs. He told me how ridiculous the system was. He could get $200,000 in unsecured student loans but couldn't borrow $60,000 to start a business with a guaranteed source of repayment. It's these sorts of practices that have made college so much more expensive than it used to be. Universities know the money is out there, and they don't worry about raising tuition. They know kids can just borrow and get the money. But in the end, we have another government-induced problem because we have made student loans so easy to get that default rates are soaring. Who winds up paying for those defaults? The same government that is already in debt over its head.

I visited one high school recently that had 1,300 students. I asked the principal how many were going into vocational programs, and he said twenty-nine. I said, "Are you telling me 1,271 students in this school are being prepped for college?" He said yes. I told him he was really preparing many of them for a financial disaster. He told me the school gets paid by the state government based on the number of students it trains for college.

That, he said, is just how the system works. Yeah, I thought, it's a system designed by politicians.

The problem is we are pushing all kids to go to college because that's the government system, even if college isn't right for many of them. It's yet another political problem that will trigger a bailout, and when that happens, the same politicians who helped cause the problem will be the ones voting to spend taxpayer money to fix it.

When I was in high school, we had a certain number of required "vo-tec" classes, which taught us practical life skills. I had to make a shelf in wood shop and a hammer in metal shop. I also had to take home economics, where I learned to sew my own shirts and make my own breakfast.

Today, many of those programs are gone, or available only at certain schools. At the high school I visited, the principal told me that few kids take vocational classes because they had to be bused to a different high school — the only one in the district that offered them. There was a stigma that made them feel less adequate compared with everybody else. And that's not their fault. It's our fault. Government created this system, fueled by education funding and overly generous student loans and grants, that makes college the only acceptable choice for high school graduates.

This is going to cause even bigger problems for colleges, because the population is shrinking. Even though more kids coming out of high school now go to college, there are fewer kids coming out of high school. With the rise of the millennial generation, colleges could be very selective. Now, you're getting to the point where you're bringing in everybody you can. Some of those students shouldn't be there, and they're failing. Even those who manage to stay in school often take longer to graduate. Employers increasingly question the value of a college education because they must do so much remedial work with today's graduates in basic skills like writing and finance. What's more, everybody involved in this system — the enrollment administrators, the federal loan officers, even the college admissions counselors — have to keep their numbers up. You don't become a successful admissions officer with declining admission rates. This looks a lot like the run-up to the housing crisis — a lot of people are making money on the volume of student loans, student applications and university attendance, but fewer people are going to earn back the investment they make in a college degree. And behind that giant, jerry-rigged construct is a federal government that makes borrowing easy, makes failure easy and makes any other option difficult. It's not going to end well.

As with so much else that the government does, no one looks at the long-term consequences. A recent analysis by the Federal Reserve found that the average student loan debt held by those between the ages of twenty-four and thirty-two doubled to $10,000 between 2005 and 2014. By the way, homeownership fell by 9 percent during the same period. While the biggest debt carried by most baby boomers and Gen Xers was their mortgages, for millennials of the same age, it's student loans. In other words, faced with paying off college loans, fewer millennials are buying homes. It's not just about saddling young people with crippling debt. We're sowing the seeds for slower economic growth in the future. If the burden of college debt causes people to stop buying homes and starting businesses of their own, the economic impact will be profound.

What makes it worse is that it's so unnecessary. In Ohio, you can still make a good living in careers like welding. There is dignity and opportunity in vocational skills, yet that message does not come through to the kids. They are told the only dignity lies in going to college. But welders can make more money than many college graduates, and they're in demand. Companies can't find enough of them because nobody's taking the classes.

In the end, we need to remember that the educational system is the result of political choices. Our political system has chosen to emphasize certain career options and career paths and basically drawn the curtains on other options. While it showers higher education in cheap money, the government is creating a different kind of crisis at the primary level. The Department of Education believes everything should be standardized. When I first got to Congress, I brought in superintendents from around the country — Louisiana, Texas, California — and they all said that standardized tests weren't improving education because all kids learn differently. Every school is a different environment, a different learning atmosphere and different kids. It's impossible to account for all those variables. But again, our education system is driven by politics. Politicians believe they can improve schools by mandating standardized tests and using the scores to rate the educational systems against each other. The politicians believe they know how to drive these outcomes better than the educators. But many of the programs Congress developed are based more on the wishes of donors whose money politicians need to get reelected, rather than on driving outcomes that would benefit school children.

Our country has different regions with different philosophies. The way you learn in Louisiana may not be the same way you do in Ohio or California. The superintendents I spoke with all said that teaching should not be standardized. Our children are not robots to be programmed the same way, and our educators need the flexibility to interpret the curriculum for the needs of the students. Setting regimented nationwide criteria for all students doesn't improve education. The best way to measure the quality of education is to assess where a student is academically at the start of the year, then do the same at the end of the year and compare the difference. This would show individual progress. Unfortunately, it's hard to quantify across the entire student population, so politicians who want to be able to say they improved education can't get the political boost they're looking for. So, we use mechanisms that give us a single score or benchmark that politicians can tout, even if our students aren't actually better off.

ᴙ ᴙ ᴙ

Some government-created crises have more immediate economic impact. One of the most egregious examples in the past eight years — and it was also one of the biggest budget busters at the time — was what's known as the "doc fix" for Medicare.

The bill was designed to change permanently the way Medicare paid doctors. In 1997, Congress passed a bill that was supposed to slow Medicare's growth by limiting reimbursements to doctors. As a result, hundreds of doctors around the country threatened to stop accepting Medicare, and Congress responded by blocking the payment reductions every year. The doc fix blocked cuts in Medicare payments and provided financial incentives for doctors to bill based on a patient's overall care, rather than for each office visit.

As often happens, it was passed amid a crisis. The Centers for Medicare and Medicaid Services, which administers payments, was just days away from cutting the rates for doctors. Of course, because it had to be done in a hurry, it was voted on by unanimous consent without any of us actually voting for it. Under unanimous consent, the leadership sets the terms for considering a specific bill and limits the time for debate. As a result, the doc fix never even went through committee. I was on the Ways and Means Committee, and we should have had the opportunity to meet and vote on it. Instead, it went right through the system untouched by amendments or even an actual vote. It was put on the floor when no one was in the chamber to debate it. It was timed perfectly by leadership.

Ironically, in 2018, when I was running for the Senate against Sherrod Brown, he got an endorsement from physicians' groups in Ohio because he claimed he had helped draft the doc fix bill. It was just another example of a politician laying claim for something he really didn't do. John Boehner and Nancy Pelosi put the doc fix bill together and put it through the House on unanimous consent, and it went to the Senate and was passed and signed by the president. Brown didn't write the bill, but he took credit for it. The bill was whisked through the process, and then when Obama signed the bill, he praised Congress' bipartisanship in passing it. For most of us in Congress, we were standing on the platform, watching the train race past.

So, Congress takes credit for working together to pass a bill that "improves" Medicare, which makes lawmakers look good to the public and makes doctors happy. But the real losers are the future doctors and patients — our grandchildren. Because rather than trying to fix the really big problem of Medicare costs, we just keep adding onto them with these quick fixes.

What all these examples showed me was that the reason Congress couldn't see how its actions could lead to a crisis was because no one understood, or bothered to acknowledge, the lack of financial controls in government.

This isn't a political party issue. Neither side gets anything done. When I was in the House, I saw firsthand why this happened. In any given session, we might pass 350 bills out of the House, but the Senate would take up only fifty or sixty of them. Of those, it would pass the ones that were addressing an impending crisis, but they would largely ignore anything that dealt with a long-term issue. Instead, we ran the country by lurching from crisis to crisis.

Members of Congress just assume that the money will keep flowing, and it will always be so abundant that we should use as much as we can. In business, you make decisions for the long term. I sit on the board of a company, and the CEO said he wanted to buy a piece of equipment that cost $250,000 and that it will save $280,000 a year for ten years. That was a no-brainer, because the long-term benefit justifies the short-term expense. Sometimes, the payback isn't there, so we nix the idea. In Washington, no one looks at the long-term payout. They just spend the money.

9

FAILURE
OF LEADERSHIP

Harry Truman famously declared "the buck stops here." He accepted that responsibility because, after all, it did. Well, as I've made it clear through these many pages, the way things work now, everything good and bad that happens in Congress rests at the feet of the party leaders. That may not be how our Founding Fathers wanted things or how we want them today, but that's how it is. And so, if you're a Republican voter or an independent or a Democratic voter who thought the GOP would do the right thing when it had power, you can know this: The blame for the GOP's Lost Decade ultimately rests with the GOP's leaders in both houses of Congress.

That said, those leaders were in a tough spot. During my time in the House, I served under two speakers. They both faced the same problem: how to deal with the far-right faction of the party. The Tea Party, which morphed into the Freedom Caucus, was made up of a lot of my fellow freshmen who came to Washington in 2010 with big plans for change. They had an innate distrust of the Washington establishment, and that included leaders in their own party. This set up a showdown between the old guard and the new. Whoever won was going to control the agenda.

You'd think that the speaker of the House would hold all the cards since they control the committee assignments, what bills come to the floor and pretty much everything that passes through that side of Congress. But, in fact, being speaker is like being a circus ringmaster, juggler and lion tamer at the same time. Technically, the speaker represents the entire House, not just one party. In fact, every time a speaker is elected, both parties put forth candidates. Of course, the minority party candidates have no chance of winning, because it's almost always a party-line vote. So, even though theoretically the minority party could influence the election of a new speaker, it really doesn't. That means the speaker must appeal to a majority of their own party, which is where the role of lion tamer comes in.

John Boehner rode the wave of the 2010 election into the speakership, but he had been around Washington for twenty years by then. His political path was fairly traditional. He started out in local politics, serving on the board of trustees for Union Township, north of Cincinnati. From there, he won a seat in the Ohio House and then used that to springboard to Congress.

He didn't waste any time cozying up to power. His freshman year, he was one of then-Speaker Newt Gingrich's Gang of Seven, which set to work investigating several House scandals, including one involving the Congressional Post Office that led to the indictment of longtime Democratic Congressman Dan Rostenkowski, who was once considered one of the most powerful people in Washington. Boehner also helped draft Gingrich's Contract with America, a platform that in 1994 helped Republicans win a majority in the House for the first time in four decades.

In 1995, Boehner entered the Republican leadership ranks behind Gingrich and Texans Dick Armey and Tom DeLay. He later helped lead a coup against Gingrich, which ultimately resulted in him being replaced as speaker by Dennis Hastert. In 2005, after DeLay was indicted and resigned as majority leader, Boehner replaced him, campaigning as a reformer who would take a hard line on spending. Ending earmarks was one of his rallying cries.

But his leadership was cut short by a shift in the political winds. The Republicans had grown unpopular largely because of the failures of the war in Iraq, and Democrats put forth candidates who could appeal to moderate voters across the country. In 2006, the Democrats swept to majorities in both houses of Congress and Boehner became a minority leader. Four years later, as voters tired of President Obama's agenda, the GOP won back the majority — and I was part of that story. Boehner was elected speaker, and the GOP had a shot at governing again. While I bristled at the way he handled my initial committee assignments, I mostly got along well with him. He was a good speaker who wanted to make deals, find solutions to problems and generally do the right thing. Unfortunately, that instinct led to his political demise.

In July 2011, just months after I took office, Boehner attempted to cut a deal with President Obama. It was probably the right thing to do. We needed a deal that would change Washington, and Boehner wanted to make that happen. Obama had been wrangling with Republicans over the budget and Boehner was ready to offer some compromises to get cuts elsewhere in the budget. While both sides said they wanted to significantly reduce the deficit, neither side could agree on how. Some freshman Republicans questioned the administration's warnings about their budget ideas and bristled at raising the debt ceiling, which had to be done by early August.

When one side proposed short- and long-term spending plans, the other side shot them down. Obama and Boehner were at a standstill, and — just three years after the beginning of the Great Recession — the financial markets were getting jittery. They wanted an end to the brinkmanship over the debt ceiling and the budget, and they wanted to see a path to far smaller deficits.

On a Sunday morning, while Obama was at church with his family, his advisors smuggled Boehner and House Majority Leader Eric Cantor into the White House. When Obama returned, he pulled the two Republicans into the Oval Office and proposed a debt reduction figure — about $1.2 trillion over 10 years — that Boehner believed might actually fly with the Republican membership.

That night, Boehner arranged a conference call with the rank-and-file members like me. When he revealed that he had secretly met with Obama at the White House, many of the Tea Party newcomers were incensed. In some ways, I didn't blame them, but I trusted Boehner to negotiate a final plan, even though it was yet another violation of regular order. Policy was being crafted by party leaders in closed-door sessions at the White House. The big problem for Boehner was his members were impatient. They wanted to know exactly what was being negotiated, and he wasn't comfortable giving out all the details. I didn't blame him. In Washington, nothing is a secret. Whatever he would say would be leaked to the press within the hour. We were left waiting to be told what the policy would be, and we were expected to support it. It was clearly a blatant example of how top-down the leadership had become. Even worse, we were being told to trust Obama on spending. Few in the Tea Party believed he would keep his promise to make such deep cuts. As members pressed Boehner, he became more vague about the plan's details, further undermining the Tea Party's confidence in his leadership. As their concerns became public, more people started questioning what Boehner was doing. The plan seemed half-baked, and what's worse, it didn't represent the views of the people who voted us into office.

Republicans had won significant victories in Congress just months earlier, largely because we promised greater accountability over federal spending and deficits. We had a political mandate to change things up, and Tea Party members, in particular, they didn't feel they needed to give any ground. The will of the people, as they saw it, was behind them. Besides, even though Obama appeared to want to deal, he kept moving the goalposts. It looked to us like he had more interest in neutering Boehner than in actually solving the problem. In the end, the entire deal unraveled. The so-called Grand Bargain evaporated in a matter of days, and with it went any chance that Republicans would trust Obama again or that Obama would work with Boehner anymore.

But while the fiscal condition of the nation was bruised and Obama didn't get to reach a deficit reduction deal he could live with, Boehner was damaged, too. The Tea Party folks blamed him for setting up this failure. His clandestine meetings with the White House put the Republicans in a terrible position of looking like they were seeking a deal they couldn't actually deliver on. From that point forward, the members who came in on the strength of Tea Party voters became Boehner's nemeses. A few years later, many of those members would become his biggest obstacles to change. They formed what is now called the Freedom Caucus and set their sights on Boehner. Four years later, a Tea Party–style candidate ran in a primary against Cantor and beat him; a year after that, Boehner resigned as speaker. He never really gave his reasons for resigning, but most people knew the Freedom Caucus kept him awake at night.

It's worth noting that while the Freedom Caucus shaped the GOP's political majority for the decade, its only major victories were these resignations. Yes, the political careers of Boehner and Cantor were cut short, but the federal government kept getting bigger, the deficit grew larger and the rest of the Tea Party agenda sat on the sidelines.

🐘 🐘 🐘

Boehner's fundamental mistake was believing he couldn't corral the far right and keep them contained. His leadership style was to ignore them, which didn't end well. They fought him at every turn and even threatened to file a motion to vacate the chair and call a new election for speaker. On August 4, 2015, Mark Meadows actually filed the motion but referred it to committee instead of making it a privileged resolution. If he had made it a privileged resolution, it would have required calling for a vote. Most people, including Boehner, realized the Freedom Caucus would control the vote and he wouldn't survive. Although he never acknowledged it, it clearly played into his decision to resign. He, like so many longtime Republicans in Washington and around the country, failed to properly understand the emotion-

al appeal of the Tea Party movement, not to mention its vola-
tile character. These were longtime Republican voters, but they
were tired of Republican politicians who seemed too quick to
cut deals and settle into Washington's cozy culture of the con-
nected. They wanted bomb-throwers and desk-tossers. People
like John Boehner and his successor as speaker, Paul Ryan, just
didn't have it in them.

On the way out, Boehner hand-picked his successor — yet
another tactic that circumvented regular order. Boehner always
believed Eric Cantor would be his successor, but after Cantor's
unexpected defeat in 2014, no one knew who was next in line.
Boehner didn't want to leave without promoting his successor.
Ultimately, he chose Ryan, who was chairman of the Ways and
Means Committee. We didn't know it at the time, but Boehner
later wrote that he had secretly groomed him for the job.

Ryan was a Wisconsin native who studied economics at Miami
University in Oxford, Ohio. A career politician, he interned for
Wisconsin Senator Bob Kasten while he was still in college. (He
also volunteered for John Boehner's campaign.) After college,
he took a job writing political speeches for former vice presidential candidate Jack Kemp and others and then became legislative
director for then-Congressman Sam Brownback of Kansas. He
was first elected to the House in 1998, and he would be reelected
eight times.

A self-proclaimed deficit hawk, Ryan served four years as chair
of the Budget Committee starting in 2011, succeeding Bachus.
Everyone always believed that Ryan wanted to focus on the kinds
of big meaty issues that interested him most: reforming the tax
code, reducing the tax impact on wages, jobs and investment,
bringing real reforms to federal spending on entitlements, and
so on. Even though Ryan gained massive exposure and a lot of
admiration among Republicans while serving as Mitt Romney's
running mate in 2012, nobody was surprised when he indicated

he didn't want to be speaker after Boehner's resignation. Instead, he supported someone else, Kevin McCarthy. I give Ryan credit for not wanting to upset the apparent succession plan. The Freedom Caucus, though, and many others opposed McCarthy because he had been part of Boehner's leadership team. Many of the caucus members believed he would just be another Boehner. Under pressure, McCarthy withdrew his candidacy.

Ryan's name came up as a compromise. He said he wasn't sure he wanted the job and asked for a weekend to think about it. That day, as I was heading home, I ran into Ryan at Reagan National Airport in Washington as we were both flying out on a Friday afternoon. I congratulated him, but he said it was too soon for that. He told me he was taking the weekend to decide if he wanted the job. He seemed unsure. Ryan's focus in Congress had always been tax reform and reducing spending, and by then, he had finally achieved his longtime goal of chairing Ways and Means, which put him in a key position to implement his ideas. I don't believe he really wanted to be speaker. I think he would have preferred to remain chairman of Ways and Means because he's a policy wonk, and he really wanted to lead the charge on tax reform. I told him, "If you don't want it, don't take it. It's not worth taking the job just because others want you to. You have to want it." I also said, "Taking it could be the biggest mistake you could make, and it could come back on you and be a problem." And that's exactly what happened.

He took the job, largely at Boehner's urging. Boehner didn't want to see control of the party turned over to the Freedom Caucus, and he thought Ryan could reunite the party factions. Ryan was elected speaker in late October 2015.

He took a different approach to the far-right wing of the party than Boehner. While Boehner sought to keep the Freedom Caucus out of his inner circle, Ryan welcomed them in. In fact, to assure his votes for speaker, he agreed to give them seats on some of the more powerful committees like Ways and Means and Energy and Commerce. He was clearly trying a new strategy with the same group that had basically ousted Boehner. In the end, it didn't really make much difference.

Giving the far right a seat at the table just provided them the opportunity to block initiatives before they were brought to House members rather than after. This had the effect of closing off any kind of dynamic discussion of key issues among the party's members, and it made people like me feel as though we weren't being taken seriously. I don't blame the Freedom Caucus for advancing their point of view, but if you're someone with different ideas, the speaker owes it to you to let you have your say when it comes to setting the agenda. You've got to run the House like you would a business, which means listening to all sides. In this case, Ryan indulged with the far right, thereby alienating those of us closer to the center, and he had no goodwill among Democrats at all. A more adept speaker would have tried to counterbalance the Freedom Caucus and force them to make concessions every so often by delivering negotiated agreements regularly so that each major faction had a good reason to stay at the table. Instead, the only faction that mattered was the one that had Ryan's ear — the Freedom Caucus. And when that faction collapsed in political power, Ryan didn't have anyone to lean on.

Ryan's successor, Nancy Pelosi, may be making a similar mistake. She's bringing the far left into the fold, giving key committee assignments to Alexandria Ocasio-Cortez and Ilhan Omar. But these new members have their own celebrity and following, and, in a sense, Pelosi may owe them more than they owe her. They are just like the Freedom Caucus in its earliest days — they have a political mandate and energy, and they regard anyone who stands in their way as someone to steamroll, not negotiate with. They're not wrong. Right now, they have the momentum and the power, but one day, they won't. Pelosi has to ask herself whether by indulging the far left rather than corralling them, she will have sown the seeds of destruction for her own party's future control of Congress. When the extreme wing of a party dictates direction, the voters eventually notice, and the response can be swift and brutal. If Pelosi doesn't want to suffer the same fate as her predecessors, she had better learn that lesson soon.

Boehner always said it was important for the speaker to remember that he or she represented the entire House, not just one party. Their job was the smooth functioning of the body, not partisan gain. In reality, though, it's impossible to separate the two. Boehner couldn't, Ryan couldn't, and it doesn't look like Pelosi can either. It's an inherently political job, and in a time of deep political division like we have now, the speaker winds up getting blamed for everything — the inaction, the division, the partisanship and anything else that people dislike about Washington. That happens to be one reason why no sane person should ever take the job of speaker of the House.

10
POLITICS AS USUAL

Failure of leadership was on full display during the 2017 budget session, which was my last time to go through the process. At one Republican-only Budget Committee meeting (remember, when it's not a formal hearing, the parties meet separately), I gave an impromptu speech to my freshman colleagues. I told them:

"I hope you never forget what I am about to say. And seven years from now, I hope you remember me as well. I came here in 2010 with almost ninety new Republicans and a mandate that we were going to change Washington. Our debts and deficits were at record highs. We were going to change the process, and we were going to balance the budget, and we promised ourselves that we would not put ourselves in the situation that we were in in 2010. Seven years later, we not only have not balanced the budget, we've broken the budget four times, we've spent more than we ever spent, and our deficits are growing. We failed because we were not willing to do what was right. We were not willing to cut spending, we were afraid of losing the majority, and we are now passing over twenty-plus trillion dollars of debt. I'm leaving after this cycle, but you now will have the mantle of not allowing the debts and deficits to grow. Don't be here in seven years asking yourself, 'Who was that guy seven years ago who told us to not fall into the same trap?' We failed, and I hope you don't for the sake of our children and grandchildren. We can change things this year. We can cut mandatory spending and make a difference."

Nobody could argue with me about these points. Tom Cole, a senior member from Oklahoma, backed me up and told them I was right. Several of the freshmen later came up and thanked me for speaking out. For me, it was a defining moment.

Unfortunately, when I visited the house in early 2019, I found that most of those members had moved off the Budget Committee. Nothing had changed. Everyone still wanted off the Committee of the Damned as quickly as possible. It's a shame, because it's the committee that should have the most power, but it has the least. I found one of those freshmen I spoke to in 2017, who had moved to another committee, and he told me he felt like he was wasting his time on Budget. It was par for the course. Nothing was going to change. After all, the Class of 2010 came in with the promise of changing our federal spending habits and we didn't change anything.

In 2017, we broke through the very modest constraints we put on ourselves through sequestration, and the budget began bloating again. It's not a coincidence that the deficit is now as big or bigger than it was in 2010. Like so many other rules that Congress makes for itself, sequestration was just another mandate that Congress created and then decided not to follow.

Maybe I was naïve, but in 2017, I had hoped it would be different. We had another opportunity to change things. We had a Republican president, a majority in the Senate and the political mandate to do what we had promised to do but which Obama didn't allow us to do. Nobody could stop us, realistically, from anything — nobody, it seems, but ourselves. The president wanted a tax cut and jobs bill, and to do that, all we had to do was pass a budget. The Senate would have to pass one, too. Then we could use a process known as reconciliation to get the various committees to lower taxes and cut mandatory spending. We finally had a chance to make a difference. All of those adjustments would have been rolled up into an omnibus bill and voted on by the full House and Senate. The process allows the budget to pass with a simple majority vote, getting around the sixty votes required in the Senate to close debate and allow a bill to come to a vote. (The Affordable Care Act, by the way, was passed in the same manner.)

We finally have a chance, I told the Republican freshmen, to change the way we're spending money. What we need to do, I said, is look beyond the 15 percent slice of the pie we'd focused on for years and focus on the mandatory spending of our entitlement programs — Medicare, Medicaid and Social Security, but also the so-called mandatory spending in each committee. The Agriculture Committee, for example, has a program like food stamps that's considered untouchable. Every committee has programs like that, and we needed to look at them all. I proposed that we come up with a number by which we could cut mandatory spending across the board.

Budget Committee Chair Diane Black said she would go to all the other committees and ask them what mandatory spending they believed they could cut. She came back with a total of about $500 billion over a ten-year period. They wouldn't guarantee it, but they'd consider it. I held up the sheet with the list of potential cuts and told the freshmen, "This is a starting point," but I had to concede, it was a pretty bad starting point. Cutting $500 billion over ten years meant we were committing to only $50 billion a year — just a tad over 1 percent of the $4 trillion federal budget. I wanted to dig deep, but they were only skimming the surface. Meanwhile, even the cuts they were offering up were illusory. Over 10 years, anything can happen. Most committee chairs don't expect to be in their position in a decade, so when they pass their current appropriations, they cut nothing but promise to make cuts the next time or the time after that. "Don't let them kid you," I told the freshmen. "This is a great starting point, but it means nothing." At least, I thought, we could finally send a signal that we were doing something.

We would be better off, I said, cutting $50 billion immediately rather than $500 billion over a decade. But it didn't matter anyway, because when Black took the $500 billion in cuts to the Republican leadership, they refused to support it. They worried that once they pledged to cut that much, they would actually have to do it, so they proposed cutting only $12 billion over ten years. It was, in the great scheme of things, like a drunk saying he'll give up booze — on February 29. It didn't mean a thing.

I was furious. Why were we being forced to negotiate with our own leadership? Our job as the Budget Committee was to pass a budget that we believed was right. So, Black went back to party leaders and committee chairs and negotiated $110 billion in cuts over ten years — one-fifth of what we knew we could do. I knew what would happen. Nothing would be cut in the first two years, and by then, the makeup of the Budget Committee would change. The newcomers would lower the amount of the cuts, and, ultimately, nothing meaningful would happen. Again, I argued for cutting $20 billion right away, but I was overruled.

That's when the fun really began. We started a hearing to approve the budget, which is a day-long process that ends with a roll call vote that starts with the most senior members and goes to the most junior. Remember, this is just Republicans, because the Democrats are meeting separately. We knew they would all vote against any budget we proposed. I didn't want to lose the opportunity we had. With Congress actually passing a budget for the first time in years, I wanted to use this chance to extract meaningful cuts. I could feel it slipping away, but I also knew it wouldn't take many of us voting against the proposal to kill it. We wanted at least the $500 billion in cuts, and we certainly could get that by voting down the current budget in committee.

I was frustrated. During a break, I spoke in the hallway with several other committee members who agreed: David Brat of Virginia (who had beaten Eric Cantor and was a true Tea Party believer), Matt Gaetz of Florida, and Glenn Grothman of Wisconsin. We were talking about how we really should stand our ground and vote against the budget. We all wanted to approve the reconciliation bill so we could get the tax cuts, but we also wanted to take a bigger bite, for the first time, out of mandatory spending.

Gaetz was the least senior member, which meant he voted last, and he told us that if the rest of us voted no, he would too.

Brat and Grothman were both senior to me on the committee, and I told them I was a no vote as long as they were. I wanted to see deeper cuts, but I wasn't going to be the only person voting no if the bill was still going to pass.

I turned to Grothman and asked him if he'd vote no first so we could all follow him. He typically wasn't very vocal in the committee and shared our views. He often appeared disheveled — wrangled shirt, tie askew — but he's smart, and he knew we had a problem. He was also from Wisconsin, which was Speaker Paul Ryan's home state. We're all staring at him, and he has sweat rolling down his face. I thought he might have a heart attack. He said, "I know I should vote no; I know I should vote no, but I'm going to have a tough race. The speaker told me he'd help me, but I better vote yes on this budget."

"You're selling out to the Cheese Man?" Brat asked, referring to Ryan. Grothman looked at the floor and just kept saying "I know I know I know." Finally, Brat said, "I'm not cutting my own throat if he's going to vote yes."

"Look," I said, "I told you, you three vote no, I vote no. But if you two don't vote no" — I pointed at Brat and Grothman — "we already know everybody else is a yes. This bill's going to pass, and if we vote no" — I pointed to myself and Gaetz — "we're going to look ridiculous."

When the vote came down, Brat voted yes, Grothman voted yes, so did I and so did Gaetz. We had been tripped up by my third rule of government dysfunction: Politics got in the way. Members may have firmly held views, but there is no power as great as the force that drives elected leaders to do anything to reassure their job security. And that means doing whatever leadership wants. Even Dave Brat, who defeated one of the top Republicans in the House, lived by that rule.

We passed the budget with the $120 billion in cuts, but it didn't matter. We were lying to ourselves, because in 2018, no one cared what we had done in 2017. Sure enough, the next year, we lost the House. Now, Democrats control the House, and the minuscule spending cuts we did manage to pass have already been eliminated.

🐘 🐘 🐘

During my tenure in Congress, the government shut down twice — once in 2013 and again at the end of 2018. The first one happened because the junior Republican senator from Texas, Ted Cruz, wanted to delay funding for the Affordable Care Act so that changes could be made to the law. Democrats and the Obama administration opposed the tactic. Even if I had agreed with Cruz, there was no way the sitting president — whose name was synonymous with the law — was going to go along with this stunt. The resulting standoff meant that we couldn't pass that old friend of ours, the continuing resolution, and so a sixteen-day shutdown began on October 1, 2013.

When we say the government shut down, that's a misnomer. You might even call it a useful bending of the truth. The federal government doesn't ever shut down. People still show up to work — our military, doctors and nurses in our Veterans Administration clinics, the people who issue Social Security checks, the people who guide planes in for a safe landing, and, yes, even members of Congress.

Instead, when we talk about government shutdowns, the only things affected are what's known as "nonessential services," such as national parks. That's not to say there are no consequences. During the 2013 shutdown, 800,000 federal workers were furloughed and another 1.3 million had to keep doing their jobs without knowing when they would get paid. But everybody got paid, even those who were told not to show up for work. I don't blame federal workers and the voters for hating shutdowns. But it's not the same as losing your paycheck.

In a sense, that's the problem. Nobody pays a real price for shutdowns except the citizens who are denied federal government services during the whole process. And shutdowns are expensive, because restarting all those services costs as much or more than it would have to just keep the government running. In fact, I don't believe shutdowns should happen at all. For one thing, it's our job in Congress to run the government, and if we don't do that, then we have failed in our basic duties. But the other reason I oppose them comes back to the problem with continuing resolutions — CRs.

Remember, we no longer follow proper budget procedures in Washington, so we use CRs to keep things going without a true budget or budget process. Shutdowns are yet another crisis that's manufactured by Congress. When someone wants to block the passage of a CR, they can undermine the entire funding mechanism for the government. The time to oppose funding measures isn't after the process is done, which is essentially what happened in 2013. The far right, led by Cruz, believed the shutdown was a good thing to do, to send a strong message about their opposition to Obamacare. But the place to address Obamacare funding was in the budget process. Since we didn't have one, Cruz opted to make a stand by opposing the CR.

John Boehner, who was speaker at the time, deserves some credit for warning Republicans that the move was a mistake. He agreed to go along with it, but he believed the party would be blamed for it, which is exactly what happened. In the end, the Republicans blinked, Congress restarted, and Obamacare remained intact — yet another air ball in the GOP's Lost Decade. The shutdown accomplished nothing except reinforcing in the minds of many voters that the Republican-led Congress couldn't do its job.

The second shutdown of my tenure, in late 2018, was different. It was also inevitable, because it was political, not financial. President Trump is committed to building a border wall, and he wanted an appropriations bill that provided $5.7 billion for it. Democrats, who had regained a majority in the House in the November elections, refused. Theoretically, Trump could have had the funding a year earlier, when we controlled the House and the Senate. But he decided to fight for the wall after the Democrats took control, and the new House speaker, Nancy Pelosi, wanted to show her fellow Democrats that she was strong enough to stand up to the president. The cynic in me thinks that both Trump and Pelosi wanted the fight more than anything else. And they got what they wanted.

Pelosi had voted for wall funding in the past, but that didn't matter. (Lots of Democrats, including Charles Schumer, Hillary Clinton, and Barack Obama, have voted for wall funding over the years.) Nevertheless, it became a political standoff. The Democrats refused to support the CR, and Trump and the Republican leadership refused to back down. A 35-day shutdown, the longest in history, began on December 22, 2018, and lasted well into the new year. Again, hundreds of thousands of government workers were furloughed and hundreds of thousands more worked without pay. The Congressional Budget Office estimated the shutdown cost more than $5 billion.

You probably won't be surprised to know that during the shutdown, members of Congress still got paid. If you hear a representative or senator proclaim that they're going to refuse their pay, don't believe them. The law requires that the government pay them. It's true, they don't have to keep the money. They can donate it to charity, which is what I did. That doesn't make me a hero. I typically donate more than one month's check to charity each year, so donating my "shutdown pay" wasn't anything noble. But the other thing is that if you take your pay and donate it, you're still taking it. Sure, the money goes to a good cause, but it doesn't address the problems that brought about the shutdown in the first place. If members of Congress really wanted to do something good with their shutdown pay, they would take the money and turn around and write a personal check in the same amount to the Treasury Department for fighting the national debt. You don't see many of them doing that. By the way, anyone can donate to help fight the national debt under a law signed by President John F. Kennedy in 1961. (You can now donate online at www.pay.gov/public/form/start/23779454. Few people do. In fiscal 2018, Americans gave only about $776,000, the lowest since 1981.)

Here's an idea: Congress should not only forfeit its own pay during any future shutdown, but it should also be forced to hand the money back to the Treasury for only one purpose: debt reduction. True, the money collected won't retire our $1.2 trillion debt to China. After all, the salary for most of the 535 members of Congress is $174,000, or $476 per day. It would take a shutdown of 4.7 million days, or nearly 13,000 years, to deal with that pile of debt! But it would demonstrate to the voters that if we don't keep the government functioning, we don't deserve to be paid at all. That's how most jobs work — you don't do your job, you don't get paid. It seems about right for that rule to apply to the people who are supposed to be in charge.

11

WAY BETTER
THAN 'A BETTER WAY'

While we didn't have a lot of victories during my tenure, we were able to pass a tax bill in 2017. To understand how we did that, we need to go back five years earlier, to when Dave Camp of Michigan was chairman of the House Ways and Means Committee. Camp wanted the committee to do a deep dive into the tax system, which he felt, correctly, was badly in need of reform. We hadn't had a major revision of the tax code since 1986. Our corporate tax rates were the highest in the industrial world, and the tax code — both for businesses and households — was a jumble of carve-outs and special breaks. It was a mess by any measure, with pieces and parts having been added over the past thirty years without anyone really taking a look at the entire system. I must admit that despite my business career and my CPA training, I appreciated the deep dive and realized many on the committee really didn't understand all the intricacies of the tax system, so the committee's work served as sort of a refresher course. Camp ultimately filed a tax reform bill that went nowhere, and he retired the next year, but his work was an important start.

In 2014, we again headed down the road to tax reform, this time with Paul Ryan leading the Ways and Means Committee. Ryan, though, had his own ideas about how the tax system should operate, so he immediately threw out the two years of work that Camp had done. Ryan had some ideas like the border-adjustment tax (BAT), the elimination of interest deductions for corporate debt and the full write-off of buildings. In keeping with the way things now work in Washington, he put together a blueprint for what he wanted his tax plan to be, and everyone else on the committee had to scramble to get up to speed. It's funny; he claimed we all knew many of these principles, but I have to admit, I didn't know what a BAT was.

I certainly agreed with the need to overhaul the tax code, but I didn't agree with all of Ryan's ideas, such as eliminating the interest deduction for corporate debt and the write-off for buildings. For one thing, I started out in my career with $200, and I wouldn't have been able to get any farther than that if I hadn't been able to borrow money from the bank. Like most businessmen, I borrowed to build my companies and create jobs. I was twenty-four years old. Some argued that I could have financed my companies through other means or found investors. They clearly had never started a business at a young age. Unless you've got a social media startup, most investors aren't going to give an unknown and untested person a chance. And most of my friends at the time couldn't have invested twenty bucks even if they wanted to. They were in the same boat, trying to make a living. Besides, when you borrow from a bank, you only have to answer to the bank, not to a slew of backers who may have different ideas about what you need to do. The bottom line is that eliminating the interest deduction meant that we would be taking away a reasonable way for building businesses. That money is used to buy equipment, hire workers, take on commercial real estate, pay suppliers, and provide goods and services that make our economy hum. All of that economic activity leads to tax revenue at the local, state and federal levels. I think most economists and tax experts would agree that you actually collect more tax revenue by allowing companies to deduct interest than you do by eliminating the deduction.

I also had concerns with the BAT. The tax basically would apply to goods where they're consumed, not where they're produced. In effect, it would mean anyone who imported goods had to pay the full tax on the items, while exporters would get a deduction on goods shipped out of the country. So, for a Walmart or Target, which imports about 95 percent of its merchandise, it would mean a new and significant tax burden and put the company at a competitive disadvantage, while for exporters like farmers, it would be a huge boon. It also meant that consumers of imported goods would be paying a higher price.

Supporters of the BAT said that retailers should find merchandise made in the United States, which sounds simple, but it would upend the entire retail business model and, ultimately, force consumers to pay more for many of the things they buy. It would have had a ripple effect through the whole economy, with many losers and some winners.

After Ryan drafted the bill and handed it down to the committee, he faced a tough sell, because a lot of the committee members weren't on board with parts of it. As 2014 rolled on, we weren't really having any hearings on the tax bill. We weren't bringing outside experts to talk about the possible impact. Instead, there was a lot of internal jockeying on the committee to try to get all the members to sign off on the basic architecture of Ryan's plan.

Then, in the fall of 2015, Boehner stepped down, Ryan became speaker, and Kevin Brady of Texas became Ways and Means chairman. Throughout 2016, leading up to the presidential election, Ryan kept working on the tax plan. It was really being crafted by Ryan and Brady, because again, everything is pushed down from the leadership. They called their proposal "A Better Way," and it was designed to reshape the way government approached issues such as poverty, national security, the economy, health care and taxes. BAT was just one of its sweeping changes.

On taxes, it replaced many of the things that I didn't like in Ryan's earlier efforts, and it included provisions to cut the corporate tax rate to 20 percent from 35 percent, repealing the corporate alternative minimum tax. However, it kept the write-off for real estate, the elimination of the interest deduction, and the BAT, which was the biggest revenue generator and would help offset declines in the corporate tax rate.

As the presidential campaigns ramped up, the Republican leadership kept trying to convince us that we should all be using the Better Way as a platform to run on, but no one did. Instead, we had seventeen candidates for president who all started attacking one another. No one was talking about a Better Way; they were all talking about their own ways. Ryan said we needed to provide leadership, and he encouraged House members to run on the plan and ignore what the presidential candidates were doing.

After the election, with the Republicans retaining the House, he started talking about passing laws as part of the plan. During 2017 we had a lot of discussion about the Better Way, but we still weren't holding many hearings — again we received no input from experts on the long-term impact of the Better Way. Instead, it was just the leadership — principally Paul Ryan — telling us what we needed to do. I make a distinction between talking about something and actually holding hearings where we might get information outside of our own biases.

Meanwhile, there was still resistance to the BAT, and once, when I came out at a Ways and Means meeting to talk to reporters, I said I didn't support it. Soon after, I was back home in Wadsworth and I got a call from a Wisconsin number. I didn't think about who it was; I just answered it. And a voice said, "Jim, this is Paul." I was caught off guard, and I said, "Paul who?"

"Paul Ryan," he said.

"Oh."

"Listen, I understand you don't support the BAT tax."

"Paul, it's just not good for Ohio. It's not good for America. It's changing the economy."

He pointed out that I really opposed only three things with the Better Way. I agreed, but those three things were significant. In Washington, we tend to forget history and repeat old mistakes. In the 1980s, we changed the tax laws to allow the fifteen-year write-off of buildings. That helped spark an office building boom. Developers in places like Houston were putting up buildings for tax write-offs only. Houston became a city with a lot of empty offices but plenty of tax write-offs. The deregulation of savings and loans around that time had resulted in a slew of bad lending practices by some S&Ls. As a result, developers had easy access to capital, and they could write off a building for fifteen years. No one bothered to ask if the building had any tenants — and many didn't. When you can write off the cost of a new building for fifteen fifteen years, you tend not to care much about whether the building is going to have any positive cash flow. You're attracted to the asset, not its return. It's a dangerous game, and sure enough, the commercial real estate market imploded in the 1980s, taking more than a few S&Ls with it. With low interest rates in 2017 (even though lending requirements had tightened after the 2009 recession), I feared we would start that chain all over again by letting people write off the full value of corporate buildings.

In the end, four of us on the committee opposed these provisions, but what finally brought an end to the Better Way was that President Trump came out against these issues as well. That stripped out most of the provisions I was concerned about, and we now were left with a purer tax reform bill. It wasn't perfect, but it was better. But we still weren't having hearings, at least not the kind where we were hearing from people that might voice any concerns. The problem with tax reform is that it's incredibly complicated and full of potentially unintended consequences. If you don't try to vet those things, the results can be disastrous.

We weren't as concerned with outcomes as we were with winning — making sure our bill got passed. We had a few hand-picked witnesses that told us the tax plan was great, and that was that. If the tax bill had had full hearings, it wouldn't have changed so quickly. Instead, we had the leadership sending around a list of the things it wanted, and then the president essentially was pulling out the things he wanted. We started in January 2017 with the Better Way, and by October, we had a whole new plan, largely based on direction from the White House. The entire process was being conducted by Ways and Means and the administration, with committee members invited to the White House to hammer out a plan.

I attended several lunches at the White House with Gary Cohn, the president's chief economic advisor at the time, and Treasury Secretary Steven Mnuchin. They were open to discussion, and they knew the Better Way plan faced resistance from the Ways and Means Committee and within the Republican majority. To their credit, they listened, took our input back to the president and contacted us regularly. They communicated with the House leadership, which began to realize that things had to change. Kevin Brady started to bring back ideas that he was getting from the White House. The dialogue resulted in changes that were more acceptable than the Better Way. In the end, that was how the tax bill — the most significant overhaul of our tax code since 1986 — was drafted.

It wasn't the way the legislative process was supposed to work. Still, I give President Trump all the credit. He wanted a tax bill, and he told his staff to work with us to get it through by the end of the year. We ended up with a different plan, and one that was not as thoroughly vetted as it should have been. It was a 1,400-page bill, and it arrived on a Sunday and we were told there would be a vote the next day. We couldn't take copies home with us because the bill hadn't been made public, so each member had about four hours to review it in a closed office. Ultimately, the "Better Way" had become "The New Way."

Despite the messy process, I defend the tax bill because it provided a long-overdue fix for our corporate tax structure. Our corporate tax rate was 35 percent. The next highest in the industrialized world was Japan at 25 percent. The United States simply wasn't competitive globally from a tax standpoint, and it was costing us businesses — which were increasingly moving their headquarters and profits overseas. Now, some people argued that the effective tax rate — the rate companies actually paid because of various write-offs and deductions — was much lower, but it was still in the 23 percent to 25 percent range. That was still the third- or fourth-highest effective rate in the world and high enough that we were losing companies to other countries.

I had been on a policy trip to Prague several years earlier, and, at the time, the Czech Republic wanted to lower its corporate tax rate and replace it with a consumption tax. I remember talking with one of the government officials at the meeting, and he said they were doing it because they hoped more businesses would come to their country. I said: "So, you're going to cut your tax rate so you can get more American companies to come here?" He replied: "If American companies come here, that's good for us, because when American companies come here, so do their payroll and their employees. Most of our tax revenue will be generated by those employees." He got the logic: Low taxes attract economic activity, which throws off tax revenue you wouldn't otherwise get. I'm not saying tax cuts pay for themselves, but tax cuts create a dynamic effect — and we should acknowledge that fact.

If you look at our federal tax system, corporate taxes account for only about 10 percent of revenue to the U.S. Treasury. We were so worried that we might be giving an unfair tax break to corporations that we forgot about the other 90 percent that comes from employees. In Prague, they didn't care about corporate taxes; they focused on the workers and consumers. Basically, they were willing to reduce the revenue coming from the 10 percent to increase the revenue coming from the 90 percent. And that results in a stronger tax base.

Our 2017 tax plan also lowered individual taxes for ten years. The reason for this was that in the 1986 reforms, we hadn't lowered the corporate tax rate, but we had created a new business entity known as a pass-through. Pass-throughs are limited liability companies, partnerships and sole proprietorships, and the 1986 law that created them allowed these types of structures to be taxed through their individual owners, at the normal tax rates they pay. By 2017, about 67 percent of businesses were being taxed as individuals. As a result, a big chunk of corporate tax revenue was now on the individual side. The only way to extend the benefits of the corporate tax cuts to these entities was to lower personal rates as well.

While I believe all of these issues needed to be done, and, as I said, I supported the bill and I still do, it came at a great cost because now we're once again running trillion-dollar deficits. We didn't fix the fundamental problems with the tax code and with the budgeting issues in Congress. There was a better way than the Better Way, and I'd been working on it for two years at that point.

🐘 🐘 🐘

The 2017 tax bill took an important step toward reducing corporate taxes, but it didn't go far enough. Back in 2015, I beefed up my House office staff with tax attorneys and CPAs. I didn't believe Congress would get serious about tax reform, and I decided to tackle it myself. We looked at changing not just the tax code but changing the entire tax system. We started by examining the tax packages of every candidate who ran for president in 2016, including Hillary Clinton and Bernie Sanders. So essentially, you had nineteen different approaches to tax reform, and while many of them had things in common, each had some ideas that were unique. We took our analysis to the Tax Foundation, which is recognized for its high-quality research on federal tax issues. With the foundation's help, we pulled pieces from each of the 19 plans, and we made a few surprising discoveries.

The biggest thing we found is that our tax system inherently limits economic growth, because the more you make, the more you pay. The system doesn't reward the hard work it takes to grow a successful business because at some point, as the tax burden increases, the business leaders simply say let's not grow anymore because we're just going to give all the upside to the government. And even if a company doesn't grow, it's taking the taxes it pays, pricing them into its products and ultimately passing those costs on to the consumer. It's really indirect double-taxation on every American citizen.

We looked at doing what the government official in Prague had mentioned to me, but we went a step further. We looked at eliminating all income tax and replacing it with a consumption tax. Instead of paying taxes when you earn and invest, we put forward a plan that would have people pay taxes only when they consume things. Then, we asked how much revenue we would need to raise to eliminate the budget deficit and run a surplus. We ran a number of scenarios, and we found that simply going after the wealthy — the fallback option most often suggested by Democrats — doesn't work, because even though they have a lot of money, there's still a limit to how much the government can expect to collect from them. After all, they can afford the best tax attorneys and lawyers, and they will find every loophole.

But eventually, we determined that a 7 percent consumption tax — an additional federal sales tax, in effect — could allow us to eliminate income tax and all corporate taxes and pay down the deficit. In other words, if everyone paid 7 percent on everything they buy, we would collect more taxes and put the country on solid financial footing, and there would be no more income taxes (people would still have to pay their Social Security and Medicare taxes, as well as state and local income taxes).

We also believed that either wages would go up or prices would go down, because companies, freed of their tax burden, would pass that on to employees or customers. If companies had an effective tax rate of 25 percent under the current system, they would see an instant profit margin increase of 18 percentage points by shifting to a consumption tax (companies, too, would pay the consumption tax on goods and raw materials they bought). Not only would we turn the deficit into a surplus, our study found that we would have one million more jobs. It also would eliminate all concerns about whether a business was a partnership or a corporation, because everyone would be paying the same tax.

I took these findings and developed my own tax plan and started showing it to other members on the Ways and Means Committee, and a number of them were interested, but they wanted to know what Ryan, who was chairman at the time, thought. I told them I didn't know because I was talking to them first. I wanted to build support for my plan the old-fashioned way — among members of the committee and then push it up to the leadership.

Of course, I soon got a call from Ryan, who had heard what I was up to, and so I had to meet with him. It was like getting called to the principal's office. He wanted to know why I was pushing my own plan because he had the Better Way, which was getting ready to roll out. I told him I thought my way was better than the Better Way. I pointed out that my plan had been developed with the help of the Tax Foundation. It wasn't long before the leadership was pressuring the Tax Foundation to drop its cooperation on my plan. And that was it. The Better Way plan moved forward, and the Renacci plan died.

Ironically, my plan had a lot of similarities with one that was introduced back in 2006. That plan, like mine, called for eliminating income tax and switching to a consumption tax. The guy who introduced that plan was Paul Ryan. When I pointed this out to Ryan — heck, I even offered to put his name on my plan — he told me it didn't work because leadership had been against him in 2006. I pointed out that he was the leadership now, but that didn't matter. I was pushing a plan that was in opposition to his new plan, and it didn't matter whether it reflected his old ideas. He had decided his new plan was better, and he wasn't going to support anything else.

What should have happened, of course, is that we should have had hearings on both plans, collected the testimony for and against each of them, carefully considered it, and then made an informed decision on which plan to put forward or looked for ways to combine them. But as I've said, that's not the way Washington works anymore. The Better Way was the leadership plan, and that's all that mattered.

Of course, my plan faced another hurdle: Politicians cringe at the mention of a consumption tax. They fear it because they don't understand it. We have long accepted that consumption taxes are inherently regressive and that they fall disproportionately on the poor. After all, if a bottle of laundry detergent costs $7, and you're making $500 a week, that's a bigger piece of your income than if you're making $1,000 a week — and if the cost goes up by 50 cents, it's a bigger hit. But what everyone forgets is that the corporate income tax being paid by companies is passed on to both the low income and the wealthy in the form of higher prices or lower wages. So, the income tax system isn't as progressive as we like to believe. If you eliminate the corporate tax, and companies are able to lower the price of goods, the impact of a consumption tax on the poor is minimized.

That's a harder message to get across, though, than sticking it to the wealthy and big companies (the typical Democratic approach) or offering a tax cut only on the margins (the typical Republican approach). As we all know, every politician is more worried about the next election than writing good bills. I still believe that in twenty-five years, something like my plan will be the law of the land. Every other industrialized economy has some sort of consumption tax. And the reason is simple: It rewards work and saving, rather than punishing it.

12

THE ROLE OF MONEY

Today's politics has an insatiable thirst for money. I knew that before I ran for office, but what I didn't understand was just how pervasive the need for money is. After I won my first election, my campaign coffers were probably about $1 million in debt, from money I lent to my campaign, so I immediately had to go into fundraising mode. Federal election laws allow the candidate to carry forward only $250,000 of campaign debt. Two months after I took office, my campaign account showed a liability to me of $250,000. I'd lost $750,000 just like that.

I wasn't as upset about that as you might think. After all, I was willing to put my own money into the race. I was mad. I'd lost my car dealership, which probably cost me a lot more than $750,000. And I believed in what I was doing. I was trying to change the country. I was proud to be a member of Congress.

But what I didn't understand at the time was that the victory — and the money it cost me — was short-lived. In less than two years, I would have to run again, and given the tight race I'd just had, I was in for another fight. All my Republican colleagues and strategists were sure the Democrats wanted to take me out.

For the first seven months after I got elected, I was fundraising every time I turned around. I kept a daunting schedule in those early months, and it was quite an adjustment. When my kids were growing up, I was home every night for dinner. After I took office, I was out of town during the week. Tina and I managed to find a new routine. I would fly home from Washington on a Friday, and we would sit down and watch episodes of *American Idol* that she had taped during the week. It was my release and a nice way for me to unwind after a week in Washington. Saturdays I might do a few things around the house and then go to mass on Saturday night followed by dinner with friends. Sunday was spent getting ready for the week ahead, and then Monday morning I'd head back to Washington.

But that was only if I didn't have any fundraising events, which I frequently did. Members often schedule "district work weeks," which are supposed to be when they meet with constituents and discuss important issues in their districts. But really, they're district fundraising weeks.

Local fundraising is just part of the money picture. In addition, the Republican National Committee holds four fundraisers a year in different cities around the country. If one of those fundraisers starts on a Friday, all the Republicans are leaving Washington on Thursday, no matter what. It doesn't matter what's going on in the government. We could be in the middle of a contentious vote. The Democrats do the same thing.

Almost from the first moment I sat down at my desk in the Cannon Building, I also had to gear up to raise funds for the next election cycle. In politics, money is a treadmill. For me, it was one that started out fast and quickly sped up.

By late spring of 2011, I got word that my district was being redrawn. Districts changed all across Ohio, but, in my case, I was told I was either going to square off against John Boccieri again or take on Betty Sutton, another Democratic stalwart. I couldn't believe it. I had already been through a tough race, spent $1 million of my own money, defeated a Democratic golden boy, and now I was going to have to do it again.

I felt abandoned by my party. Republican leaders strengthened Boehner's district now that he was speaker by shifting more registered Republican households into his district. They wanted to ensure he got reelected and wouldn't have to do much fundraising for himself. You can either be in leadership and fundraise for the party, or you can fundraise for yourself, but there's little time for both. Party leaders rarely have tough races. Often, they run unopposed in the primaries, and even if they do face an opponent in the general election, they are almost assured an easy victory. If they had to campaign and fundraise back home like the rank-and-file members did, they wouldn't have time to maintain their leadership roles. Leaders do spend time raising funds, but mostly it's campaigning for others in their party who are in tight races, which helps ensure the party maintains its majority.

In my case, though, no one was coming to help. The redistricting plan was designed to construct a stronghold for Boehner in which he was unlikely to have a challenger. His closest allies in the state got their districts shored up, too, to guarantee their continued support. I was one of the new guys, so I was somewhat on my own.

The new territory took me out of Stark County, which was staunchly Democratic but an area in which I had my strongest financial base. It was the county from which President William McKinley launched his political career. In all the years since Ohio had become a state, that county had never been divided by political boundaries — it had always sat as a whole in one congressional district or another. The redistricting plan broke the county into three pieces, and I was left with a tiny western sliver. I also lost Ashland County, which was 70 percent Republican. In its place, I received parts of Cuyahoga County, which included the heavily Democratic outskirts of Cleveland. In all, I had only about 30 percent to 40 percent of my original district left. So now, I was looking at another tight and expensive race, with a fraction of the fundraising potential and a much bluer constituency than I'd had the first time around. Even worse, there was little time for people to get to know who Jim Renacci was. As much as I tried to keep focused on the important work I wanted to do in Washington, I couldn't lose sight of this existential threat back home. I couldn't change anything in Washington if I wasn't working in Washington.

Just a few months into my first term, I could already feel the seeds of disillusionment beginning to grow. Things were not going as I'd hoped, and I'd barely gotten started. I confronted Boehner one evening as we were walking through the rotunda on our way to an event, and I complained about losing my funding base. Technically, redistricting is done by the state legislature, so Boehner couldn't admit that he'd had any influence over it, but, of course, state party officials are going to support one of the most powerful Republicans in the country. Boehner brushed off my concerns. He compared it to a church. When the parishioners like the pastor, and the pastor moves to another congregation, they follow him. "You'll be fine," he said. While I appreciated Boehner's confidence in me, I was going to have to pass the collection plate a lot more than I'd intended. Betty Sutton and I were now in the same district, and political analysts were saying it was "in play," meaning that neither of us was a clear front-runner.

We want to believe that we elect politicians to represent us, but in most cases, the decisions our elected officials make are based more on donors' money than on our actual work. So long as politicians need to keep money flowing into their campaign coffers, they will make decisions that keep that money flowing. The money is the outcome that matters — not the policy, and not the people. I know I'm not the first person to say that, but I saw it firsthand, and it's actually worse than you can imagine.

Money has transformed politics, but it's also created an entirely new class in American society. In addition to the traditional economic classes — the poor, the working poor, the working class, the suburban middle class, the wealthy — we now have the political class. Some people call them "career politicians," but I think of them as the political elite. However you define them, they are a separate set of people drawn from all the economic classes. They also are the ones who, regardless of their idealism when they first get into government, become part of the problem. It doesn't happen their first day in Washington, or their first month. Sometimes it takes years. But eventually, it happens to everyone.

You don't have to be a Republican or a Democrat to get sucked into the political class. This is an equal opportunity club. Someone from a working poor household can find their way into the political elite with the help of a well-heeled supporter. Wealthy donors lift candidates into the political class. That's what George Soros does for the Democrats, for example. How did Barack Obama, a community organizer from Chicago, or Elizabeth Warren, a Harvard professor, find the money to run for the Senate or president? Obviously, they had help. Beto O'Rourke was a small-business owner in El Paso, Texas. Alexandria Ocasio-Cortez worked as a part-time waitress and bartender in New York. O'Rourke lost his Senate race and still became a golden boy. Ocasio-Cortez was elected to the House in 2018 and even before she was sworn in, she had become Democratic party royalty. Her future is assured, even if her bank account is still light. She will never struggle for power, influence or wealthy friends the rest of her life, because she's been in Congress.

Anthony Gonzalez, who succeeded me in representing District 16 after I decided to leave Congress, entered the race as a political novice who didn't even live in the district before he decided to run. He was a standout wide receiver at Ohio State who went on to play for the Indianapolis Colts and the New England Patriots before retiring from football and getting an MBA from Stanford in 2012. In the first month after he announced his candidacy, he raised more than half a million from donors, including former NFL buddies like Peyton Manning.

Once a politician is in that elite class, they help spread the money around. They become enablers as well as recipients. And the process just keeps expanding, strengthening the political class.

Increasingly, big money is critical to the process because campaign costs have become exorbitant. Rick Scott spent almost $83 million, most of it his own money, to run for his Florida Senate seat. Meanwhile, in Texas, Ted Cruz spent $45.5 million to retain his seat against his Democratic challenger, O'Rourke, who raised almost $79 million. O'Rourke lost the race, but he secured his political future by winning the support of the political elite — and he has money. Little wonder he's running for president. He has $79 million to travel the country and campaign. Even if he spends half of that and drops out of the race, he has a hefty war chest to run for another office. A well-funded war chest is one of the best weapons you can have in politics because it tends to scare off political challengers.

That's why you can never stop raising money. Even if you have an easy race, you keep fundraising because you never know what you might face in the next race. What if an unknown billionaire decides to run against you? What if some unknown golden boy or girl suddenly shows up and captures the public's attention — and thus, the party's money? If I were John Cornyn, the senior senator from Texas up for reelection in 2020, I'd be keeping my eye on O'Rourke. Money is power. O'Rourke has no accomplishments in Washington beyond his fundraising ability. Too often, we support someone not because of their resume but because of the money they can raise. Bernie Sanders has no legislative accomplishments in thirty-five years, but he can raise money.

For me, I was allowed into the political class because I had money, but I never felt part of the elite, because I never really had the support of my party. Remember, I spent $1 million buying my way in, and after two years in office, I was redistricted into another expensive race. It was almost like the party was trying to get rid of me. Even after I prevailed in that race, I wasn't exactly welcomed in Washington. I was there to disrupt the status quo.

You can't do that and be well-liked by those who see the status quo as a way to make money.

The same process works in reverse. Ohio Senator Sherrod Brown, a Democratic darling against whom I ran in 2018, floated the idea of running for president. He raised only $100,000 in a month and he bowed out. He may be a golden boy in the Senate, but he doesn't have the fundraising clout to shoulder a presidential campaign. O'Rouke, by comparison, raised $6 million in less than a week after he announced he was running for president. I'm no fan of Brown, but when it comes to political accomplishment, he was far more impressive than O'Rourke. The problem is that the political elite don't support accomplishment. They support sizzle. Brown doesn't have it, and O'Rourke does.

Ironically, joining the political elite doesn't require any real skills or accomplishments. I served in Congress with O'Rourke. He didn't pass any bills and he rarely showed up for committee meetings, but he's obviously good at campaigning and raising money. Bernie Sanders has written one bill the entire thirty-five years he's been in Congress, but now he's running for president. Increasingly a lack of political experience is a benefit. If you didn't sponsor any bills or take any controversial votes, your opponent can't use them against you. In business, if you didn't perform the basic tasks of your job, you'd be fired. In politics, you get to try for a promotion.

Once you're anointed by the elite, then your past votes or your track record don't matter anyway. Obama took positions as president that contradicted votes and positions he'd taken earlier in his career, but nobody remembered them because he didn't leave a ripple in Congress. O'Rourke learned the lesson: In Washington, nobody cares what you once did, so long as you never did anything that ever mattered. Once you try to do something that will have an actual impact on the lives of Americans, watch out — you just painted a bright-red target on your own back.

Today, it doesn't matter how many pieces of legislation you sponsor or pass into law. All that matters is how much money you raise. Ironically, Democrats — the party that paints Republicans as beholden to moneyed interests — love this. Sanders boasts about his individual donations of $20 or less. This is all marketing hype. It makes it look as if the candidate isn't beholden to big donors, but in fact, the grassroots giving is just a small piece of what they need to run a successful race. Even with the reach of social media, shilling for a sawbuck here and there on the internet isn't going to propel you to victory. In our Senate race, Brown used to claim that he had 200,000 donors who gave him $25 apiece. Well, that's nice, but that's only $5 million. Where did the other almost $23 million he spent on the race come from? He had big money coming in from somewhere. To win a Senate seat these days in a state with few major media markets, you need $40 million or $50 million. You can't wait on all the $5 donations to trickle in. Someone, with access to big money, has to lift you up.

By the way, if you only have twenty bucks to give to a politician, save your money. Regardless of who's in power, the poorer you are, the more likely you are to be hurt by government programs. Sixty percent of Americans have less than $1,000 in the bank, which means they don't have much to protect themselves if they have a medical emergency or some other unexpected crisis. They're just fighting to move forward, and every day is a struggle. But politicians use them to stay in power. They don't really care about the poor. At the very least, those $5 and $10 donations don't give you a seat at the table or a voice with the candidate. All it does is leave you $5 poorer. Save your money and spend more time thinking about how you'll vote in the next election. That's where your impact can actually be felt.

I know there's a lot of cynicism about our politics, and I'm not telling you something that most people don't already believe.

But here's the issue: It's worse than you think. In 2018, we saw Russian hackers try to influence the election, and the tight presidential race touched off cries to abolish the electoral college. But the real threat to the integrity of our elections is the political maneuvering that happens behind the scenes — all of it legal and all of it in plain sight. Just as I saw in my early meetings with Republican county chairmen before my first race, the political elite decide who gets to run, who gets to have a shot at winning and even who gets to vote. When they redistricted me, it was their own way of taking my supporters and handing them to someone else. That's how it works. Voters don't realize their choices have been limited, influenced and altered. The political elite set the rules of the game, decide who gets to play and, in many cases, who is going to win.

That's why Donald Trump broke through in 2016. Love him or hate him, you can't deny why he would appeal to voters who were tired of being handled by the political elite in both parties. Look where his victory came from: Voters in Pennsylvania, Ohio, Michigan and Wisconsin who had voted for Democrats (or nobody) for years turned around and voted for a Republican candidate who didn't sound like all the other Republican candidates. They liked him and they liked the fact that the political elite hated him. Say what you will about the guy, but he read the mood of the country perfectly, and he beat the system.

Yet two years later, even after seeing that play out, the Republican Party — still dominated by political elites — ignored Trump's victory strategy. As I'll discuss later, in my 2018 Senate race and even today, the Republican Party largely ignored the voters in the states Trump had flipped from the Democratic column. In fact, Republican Senate Majority Leader Mitch McConnell of Kentucky has said the party was focused on other, less populated areas. It raises the question of whether McConnell wants Trump to get reelected. The political elite didn't want Trump in 2016, and they don't want him in 2020. His propensity for blunt talk, which resonated with average voters, propelled him to victory despite the elite's opposition.

Before I ran for the Senate, I entered the 2018 race for Ohio governor, and I met with a senior state Republican official who told me I was the most qualified among the four primary candidates. After the campaign started, and the other candidates were attacking me with many of the same unfounded claims that have dogged me for most of my time in politics, I asked him what I should do. You should stay in, he said. I was the most qualified, and the fact that they were all coming after me meant the other candidates knew it. But after two of the primary candidates merged their campaign, he told me to get out of the race. The surviving opponent now had the money and the backing of the political elite. Even though I was more qualified, the political machine decided it wanted somebody else. Message received. Much as I would have liked to have proven them wrong, the circumstances changed when the Senate candidate stepped away with just eleven months left in the election and the White House asked me to fill that void.

If you don't have money before you join the political class, it will help you get it. Barack Obama came to Washington with a net worth of only a few hundred thousand dollars. Today, he's worth millions. Obama and his wife, Michelle, have written books and hit the lecture circuit, where speeches from big-name politicians, including former presidents, can run into six figures for one talk. Bernie Sanders just admitted he is now a millionaire. The Clintons, of course, raised this to an art form. Regardless of how much Hillary Clinton made on commodities trading, she's made far more as a former politician and first lady. The same is true for Republicans, of course, including Boehner. Both parties have their political elites, and they all play the same game.

Being in the political elite can be its own reward, because after you leave office, everyone wants to go into business with you and pay you to speak. The power doesn't go away, it just shifts, and it becomes profitable. As a candidate you raise money, as a member of Congress you spend money — not yours of course — and then as a former congressman you make money.

People who used to want access to you when you were in office now want to pay you to be a conduit, to provide access to and insight about your former colleagues. You get named to corporate boards, you write books, you give paid speeches. Some become lobbyists or consultants. It's almost like a pension for the political elite, and it's a way to stay in a state of wealth and power and not have to return to the farm and live out your days in obscurity.

When I went to Congress, I didn't care about the money. I'd already done well for myself. In fact, I took a significant pay cut to be in Congress at $174,000 a year. I did it to serve my country and to try to fix some of the wrongs in how the country was run. Nor did I write this book in the hope of getting rich. I wrote this book to pull back the veil on the Lost Decade of the Republican Party and to show voters why the party in power didn't accomplish anything. But I'm not expecting to make a dime on this book.

The longer you stay in power, and the more prominently you wield it, the more money you can make in the political afterlife. One way to cement that staying power is to go on TV as much as possible. It used to be that the chairman of Ways and Means was one of the most powerful people in the House after the speaker. If you needed to raise money — and every politician does — then being on Ways and Means was a good way to do it.

Today, because the budget process is dictated by the White House and party leadership, Ways and Means is no longer the seat of power. Now, the plum assignment is the Oversight Committee, because the chairman gets on television constantly. Think about the airtime that Trey Gowdy of South Carolina got during the Benghazi hearings. He's become well-known nationally, not because of any bill he's sponsored, but because the committee he ran was handling things that were in the news. In the old days, being on the Oversight Committee didn't help with fundraising. It was just a good way to make enemies with the administration and your colleagues in the House. But these days, because of the role of television and twenty-four-hour cable news, it's a good way to raise your profile — and money.

All of this is the nature of the business of politics, but as time went on, this cycle of incessant fundraising and campaigning began to wear on me. The disingenuousness and hypocrisy of the political elite began to chafe. It might have been different if I had felt as though I were accomplishing what I went to Washington to do, but I wasn't. None of us were. The class of 2010, for all its hope and ambition, had become a bust. I was getting frustrated by the intransigence that surrounded me. I didn't want to become part of the problem. I knew I would have to get out.

13

GM RETURNS

I went to Washington because of the government's role in closing my Chevrolet dealership. While that was a painful experience for me and my employees, we were told that it was necessary to help General Motors get its financial house in order, save jobs in the company, and position it for the future. Yet by late 2018, less than a decade later, the automaker was once again back before Congress, hat in hand. The company had announced it planned to close five assembly plants — including one not far from my district in Lordstown, Ohio — and cancel many of the vehicles made by those factories.

It's no secret that American manufacturing is struggling. While the changes we made in the tax code are helping American companies compete, the high costs of our regulatory environment and the automakers' unionized workforce still mean it's cheaper to manufacture outside the country in many cases. In fact, one of the reasons I opposed the border-adjustment tax was that modern manufacturing makes it extremely difficult to administer. How do you tax a vehicle that has a frame and a motor made in Mexico, which is then brought to the United States and assembled, then sent to Canada, where parts and side panels that are made in yet another country are added, and then sent back to the United States for final assembly? Deciphering the tax regime for all that, not to mention the taxes due in Canada and Mexico and coming up with a total tax bill would be almost impossible.

But GM's renewed troubles went far beyond the plight of other manufacturers — or even other automakers. All the major American car companies were struggling in 2009, but Ford didn't take a handout from the government. Today, Ford is in a much stronger financial position than GM. Four years after the bailout, it reported a quarterly pretax profit of $2.1 billion and an 18 percent increase in sales.

For one thing, Ford recognized its problems earlier than GM and Chrysler did. It wasn't just a question of anticipating the economic downturn, it was a question of recognizing shortcomings within its own ranks. Bill Ford, who was the chairman and chief executive in the mid-2000s and a scion of the company's namesake, realized the company needed to change its thinking. He brought in Alan Mulally, a former Boeing executive, to overhaul the automaker's operations.

Mulally simplified the company's cost structure, reducing the number of vehicle platforms it used worldwide, which led to big savings. He also recognized that the company needed to invest heavily in new product development. In 2006, two years before the start of the Great Recession, he literally put everything on the line. He mortgaged the company's assets — including its famous blue oval logo — and secured a $24 billion line of credit. That helped Ford weather the downturn.

Meanwhile, GM and Chrysler made no such investments or plans. When the recession hit, they went running to the government for help, warning that if they failed, it would cost one million jobs at a time the economy could least afford it. Of course, many of those jobs were union jobs, which certainly got the Obama administration's attention.

Between 2008 and 2014, the federal government shoveled almost $81 billion into the two car companies. The government essentially bought a controlling stake in both GM and Chrysler (it later sold Chrysler to Fiat). For about six years, the U.S. government actually was one of the world's biggest carmakers. It's support for GM was so great that Ford, despite not needing the handout, asked to be included in the bailout program. It argued that by not participating, it would be put at a competitive disadvantage.

It needn't have worried. The bailout didn't save GM, and it didn't, as some people like to think, work out well for the government. The government lost more than $11 billion on its "investment" in GM, and it lost $1.3 billion on the Chrysler deal. It still irks me that Obama is credited with "saving" the U.S. auto industry. He didn't, and he threw a lot of good taxpayer dollars away in the effort.

Clearly, the failure of GM and Chrysler was about more than just a decline in the overall economy or the challenges facing American manufacturing. It was about mismanagement. Unlike Ford, GM didn't retool its plants, it didn't consolidate production, it didn't cut jobs. And when it turned to Washington for help, the government was all too eager to rush in to give it.

It's worth noting that in 2001, another large corporation, Enron, made a frantic call to the White House. Its chairman, Ken Lay, argued that it was on the verge of collapse, and if it failed, it would disrupt commodities markets worldwide. Lay had known President George W. Bush for years, going back to when Bush was governor of Enron's home state, Texas. But when Lay called asking for a handout, Bush didn't take the call. Enron failed, it entered bankruptcy, and ultimately it was liquidated. Lay and his CEO, Jeff Skilling, were convicted of fraud. (Lay died before he could be sentenced, and his conviction was vacated; Skilling served twelve years in prison and was released in February 2019.) Whether Bush knew that Enron's troubles were man-made or not isn't what matters. What matters is that he understood that private companies in trouble shouldn't get a free handout from the taxpayers. They should deal with the consequences of their failure like anyone else should, regardless of their connections.

We have laws in this country that are designed to handle business failure. In fact, our bankruptcy laws are the envy of the world precisely because we treat failure in an orderly way, and we give people a chance at redemption. We are a nation built on entrepreneurship. We aren't afraid to take risks, and if we fail, we have a system that's designed to help us get back on our feet. Our bankruptcy laws allow failed companies to start over, remove inefficiencies, strip out bloated costs, and begin again. It's expensive, and it can be disruptive, but companies typically emerge from bankruptcy stronger than they were, and many go on to thrive.

Instead of owning up to its failures, GM went looking for a shortcut. And in Obama it found a president who was more than willing to take the call.

While the government's "investment" in GM ended in 2014, it had set a dangerous precedent. The bailout was poorly structured. It pumped a lot of money into the carmaker, but it didn't demand enough spending cuts, retooling, investment, and job cuts (the only major cuts were to the dealer network, which included me). The bailout allowed most of GM's inefficiencies to linger. So, four years later, guess where GM was?

In late 2018, the company's chairman and CEO, Mary Barra, came to Capitol Hill and met with the Ohio delegation. She told us GM was "unallocating" the Lordstown plant, southeast of Cleveland, as well as factories in Michigan and Maryland. "Unallocation" isn't a word; GM's lawyers created it to avoid using the term "close." Needless to say, we were unimpressed by their editorial creativity. Lordstown wasn't being unallocated, it was being closed, and the cars made there, like the Chevy Cruze, were being scrapped and so were the jobs. Barra told us the factory was operating below capacity, and that the company had more factory space than it needed to meet demand for cars and trucks. To me, that demonstrated what a failure the GM bailout was. A company just four years out of reorganization should not have bloated capacity. Obviously, the government's intervention prevented GM's management from facing the decisions it needed to make.

Barra blamed unexpected market changes for Lordstown's shuttering. Consumers wanted sport utility vehicles, and Lordstown was making sedans. I pointed out to Barra that other automakers like Honda saw the market changes coming and revamped their SUVs like the Pilot and added new models. Maybe, I guessed,

GM was slow to adapt because it was still fat from the $51 billion it got from the federal government a decade earlier.

In the meeting, the Democratic representative for Lordstown, Tim Ryan, suggested GM could make electric cars there. Apparently, he didn't realize that GM is developing electric cars elsewhere. Sure, GM wants to build electric cars, but what Barra was telling us was that the company didn't want to invest in retooling Lordstown to make them. Nor did it want to convert the plant to make SUVs or any other model. GM simply couldn't justify the cost of retooling when it had cheaper factories in Mexico. And, predictably, the Democrats in the room immediately started trying to blame President Trump. Once again, politics was getting in the way. This problem had been festering for ten years.

I told Barra that the entire reason I was even in the room was that a decade ago, her company went through what I would call a ghost bankruptcy. In a real bankruptcy, management would have been put into place with a single mission: cut costs and put the company on a firm footing to grow again. By bypassing that bankruptcy process, the government created the problems she now faced — decisions deferred, cuts not made, pain that only got worse with time. And there she was, coming back to the same government and asking for another fix. The problem is that the so-called bankruptcy didn't fix the company's legacy costs, and those costs are still dragging down the business. I told her that as a businessman I understood that she needed to do what was necessary to fix her company. "But," I said, "here is the problem I have with you: You took $51 billion and now you're going to Mexico."

She argued that the company was adding capacity at some plants in the United States, too, but the fact remained that the government intervention a decade ago and the ineffective handling by the Obama administration and GM itself will probably cost tens of thousands of American jobs. That's in addition to the six thousand jobs and 153 dealerships that were lost in Ohio alone —including mine.

By closing dealers, GM and the government hoped to reduce competition among the brand and drive prices up. When I was running my dealership in 2004, customers would come in and tell me they could buy the same car five miles away for less, and in the end, you had to match the price to stay competitive. Now, residents of Wadsworth have to drive fifteen miles to get to a Chevy dealership — and not just to buy a car but for service as well. Prices may have gone up, but it hasn't helped customers or dealers. As sticker prices rose, customers simply bought fewer new cars. That hurt dealers, and it certainly didn't help GM, either.

A decade later, we're starting all over again with a new round of GM problems. President Trump has told GM he wants the company to keep operating in Ohio, but even he can't tell a company how to run its business. He's concerned about the thousands of autoworkers in Ohio and other parts of the Midwest that have been living for years under the constant threat of plant closings and furloughs. Many of those workers looked to him for change. Unfortunately, he can't undo the bad decisions made by his predecessor.

When the government took control of the bankruptcy process a decade ago, it should have put contingencies into its loan requirements that said until the money is completely repaid, you can't increase capacity anywhere but in the United States and if you have to cut capacity anywhere, you have to cut it everywhere but in the United States. In effect, we would have insisted that GM prioritize U.S. operations over all others until the bill was paid. Instead, the Obama administration pumped in the money with few strings attached — mainly just a demand for increased fuel efficiency standards. Well, we got more-fuel-efficient vehicles, but they're being made in Mexico. That is, if anyone is buying them.

The problem with General Motors was just a symptom of the rampant dysfunction that I saw everywhere in Congress. Even before our meeting with Barra, I decided it was time for me to leave. I had come to Washington to bring much-needed change and to help my constituents, but I increasingly felt as if I was wasting my time. I wasn't getting anything done, and I knew if I didn't leave, I risked becoming part of the problem.

Those who stay too long in the broken system perpetuate the dysfunction, especially once they've shown they can raise money.

After eight years in Washington, I didn't want to go down that road. It was time to try something else. I was increasingly concerned about the dangers that congressional inaction posed for the states. After all, if the federal government couldn't get anything done, it would fall to state governments to pick up the slack. Many states, however, were still struggling with the after-effects of the Great Recession, and Ohio was definitely one of them. John Kasich had served his second term as governor and couldn't run again because of term limits. I decided that rather than run for Congress again, I would run for governor of Ohio instead.

I wanted to take my message of financial responsibility to the state level. It's as vital — and perhaps more vital — there than in Washington. Congress seems determined to keep racking up record deficits, and nobody's even talking about them anymore. When the deficit blows up, and the government can't afford to fund programs, the first thing it will do is stop sending money to the states. But nearly all states are prevented by law from running deficits. They have to balance their books each year in some way. That means that only the states that are financially strong enough to stand on their own two feet will be able to hold the Union together when the federal government collapses under the weight of all that debt.

To prepare for that possibility, we need to strengthen the states' financial positions. States that aren't solvent or, like many in the Midwest, that lack the base for economic growth, will be particularly vulnerable. Ohio is among them. Forty-two percent of the state's budget is spent on Medicaid (it used to be 17 percent). That's all dependent on money from the federal government. What happens when the feds can't do that anymore? Will we simply stop treating and healing people who are too poor to pay for their medical care? That's an unrealistic expectation, and we need a better answer. Now, multiply that across the forty states that have expanded Medicaid in recent years. It's essential that the states shore up their finances to prepare for the financial apocalypse at the federal level.

It's clear to me that this work has to be done by governors because they have the executive power to make sweeping changes. Take the example of President Trump. Not everyone agrees with his methods or his demeanor, but there's no doubt he has no compunction about making changes. He didn't keep doing things the same way just because they had always been done that way. He's a disruptor, and Washington needs more like him.

But the Lost Decade had taught me that it's easier to be a disruptor as the head of an administration than it is to be one among 435 members of the House or 100 members of the Senate. Quite simply, after eight years, I'd had enough. Despite Trump's efforts to "drain the swamp," as he liked to say, Congress was still Congress. If GM hadn't gone through its sham bankruptcy and taken my dealership away at the order of the federal government, I would just be an average citizen with a big car dealership up in northeastern Ohio. Life intervened, I came to Washington to fix that injustice, and eight years later, nothing had really changed.

That was the message from the meeting with Barra. The company was the same and the government was the same. Nobody had learned a single lesson from the incident. I almost had to laugh at the irony. I had come to Washington because of GM, and now, I would leave because of GM. The old expression applies:

History repeats itself first as a tragedy and then as a farce. I was left to wonder: In all my time in Congress, what had I accomplished in Washington?

Rather than continue in a city of farces, I decided that I could do more good for Ohioans if I was working closer to home. If I didn't win, at least I'd be out of Washington.

14

DISRUPTING THE POLITICAL ELITE

Before I ran for national office, I didn't pay much attention to presidential politics. But in 2008, a friend called me and told me that if I cared about my business, I should be concerned about the Democratic candidate, Barack Obama. I did some research, and I realized he was right. As a Republican, I obviously didn't agree with Obama's overall philosophy, nor with most of his policies. More important, though, he didn't meet the criteria that I thought were needed for a president. I believe a good president should at least have been a governor. The administrative experience gained in running a state is invaluable in the White House. My ideal candidate would be a businessperson who has some government experience.

As the 2008 race geared up, I decided to get involved, and I became an active fundraiser for John McCain. McCain lost, but I stayed involved in politics and got elected two years later to Congress. In 2012, I flew back to Ohio, endorsed Mitt Romney and became a major supporter. Romney was a business guy, but he also had been governor of Massachusetts. To me, he was uniquely qualified to be president. I believed that he could change the system in Washington.

I actively campaigned for him and became the first representative from Ohio to endorse him. Unfortunately, Romney lost, and we had four more years of Obama. In 2016, we had a huge field of Republican candidates, and many of them, quite frankly, shouldn't have been there. A few, like Rick Perry and Jeb Bush, had been governors, but they lacked the business touch. Ted Cruz and Marco Rubio were senators who'd never run anything. Of the seventeen, the only one who really stood out, given his business experience, was Donald Trump. By then, I'd spent six years in Washington, and I had become convinced that only an outsider could fix the place.

I faced a lot of pressure from Republican officials in Ohio to support John Kasich, the former governor, but it looked to me like his campaign would implode quickly. Ohioans weren't as enamored of him as they once had been. They felt he'd been too focused on running for president and had ignored the state in his second term. He'd also done some things I didn't agree with, such as overseeing the expansion of the state's Medicaid program despite the impact it would have on our state budget.

In the world of politics, it was customary for representatives to endorse a presidential candidate from their home state, but I decided to hold off. If Kasich wound up being the last man standing, I'd support him because he was from Ohio and he had the experience of being governor, but he really wasn't someone I was excited about.

The more I watched the candidates, the more impressed I became with Trump. My staff told me I shouldn't support him because he would lose, but to me, it was less about winning and more about backing the right person. The only other candidate with business experience was Carly Fiorina, the former CEO of Hewlett-Packard. Fiorina struggled with fundraising and dropped out early.

Trump continued to gain steam. He clearly was not a member of the political elite, but he had his own money to buy his way in. I could identify. As the field narrowed, my chief of staff urged me to make an endorsement, but since I didn't know Trump personally, I wanted to meet him before I offered my support publicly.

Then, someone in Trump's organization contacted my chief of staff prior to the Ohio primary and asked if I would introduce him at a rally in Cleveland. I had my chief call the Trump people back and make a deal: I would introduce him at the rally, which would essentially be an endorsement, if he introduced and endorsed me at an event in New York. Remember, in politics, you're always fundraising, and I was hoping Trump could connect me to well-heeled New York Republicans. I never really expected him to do that (and, by the way, he didn't), but I wanted to meet him in person before I endorsed him.

A few days before the Ohio primary, I got a call from Matt Borges, the chairman of the state Republican Party. Perhaps he'd heard that I was meeting with Trump. He asked me to endorse Kasich. I told him that I knew Kasich, and I'd helped him in his earlier races, but I hadn't really heard from the governor for years. Then I said, "Have Kasich call me. If he calls me, I'll endorse him." Borges said he'd have Kasich call me the next day. My chief of staff thought I was crazy. I had set up a meeting with Trump, and I just told the party chair that I'd endorse Kasich. Relax, I said. Kasich won't call back. He had a reputation for not returning phone calls. He expects everyone to call him and to keep calling him until he decides to answer them. Thinking you're too important to return calls is a hallmark of the political elite.

I'm a man of my word. I've never forgotten what my father told me before I moved to Wadsworth. If Kasich had called me, I would have endorsed him. But the day before my meeting with Trump, Borges called again and asked if I had talked with Kasich. Would I be endorsing him? I told him I hadn't heard from Kasich, and he seemed surprised. "He said he was going to call you," Borges said. He told me he would talk to Kasich again, but Kasich still never called.

The next day, Trump came to Cleveland for a rally with at least 25,000 people at the International Exposition Center. As Trump's campaign staff led me past the crowd, I assumed we were headed to a VIP reception with a hundred other people. I'd get a few minutes to meet the candidate and exchange pleasantries. That's usually how these things worked. But again, Trump didn't do things the traditional way. They led me to a back room and when they opened the door, it was just Donald Trump; the owner of the center, who was Trump's largest donor in Cleveland; and one other individual. Keep in mind, at the time, many people were afraid to publicly support Trump. The political establishment was still betting he would lose.

The meeting sealed the deal for me. While he can be brash in public, meeting him one-on-one was a different experience. I found him compassionate and thoughtful and willing to listen. "Congressman," he asked, "what do I need to win? What are the issues? What are the problems? What can I do to help you?"

He really wasn't the guy everyone was making him out to be. In that moment, I became convinced that he really wanted to fix the country. I told him I appreciated his offer and that he already had my support. I also told him he could tell others that I supported him. In fact, I told him my wife, my children, and I had all gone to the polls the day before and voted for him. And, I said, I was telling others to vote for him. That meeting, as well as the lack of a call from Kasich, sealed the deal. That day, Trump got up on stage and told the crowd, "By the way, I love your congressman here. He's a great guy. In fact, he endorsed me just now."

I had been saying for years that our next best president would not be liked because he will have to do things that are unpopular to fix our broken system. The same is true for any good politician — governor, mayor, dogcatcher. If you are making necessary — and long overdue — changes, you aren't going to be liked. I learned that as mayor of Wadsworth. At first, a lot of people, especially the Democrats, disliked me. Eventually, they respected me for doing what needed to be done. President Trump is doing the right things, which makes him disliked in many circles. That's just politics.

After our meeting at the rally, the president never forgot how I backed him in the early days of his campaign. I became a vocal supporter because the more I got to know him, the more I saw him as a disruptor, and I still believe that he's changing government for the better. He's doing a lot of things that people don't like, and he's breaking down old conventions, but that's what disruptors do. And quite frankly, it's something that's long overdue in Washington.

After he got elected, I became one of a handful of supporters who met regularly with his staff at the White House. He appreciated the fact that we had supported him early on and weren't afraid to get behind him while many in the political establishment were still hoping he would lose.

🔴 🔴 🔴

After I announced my run for governor but before my term ended in Congress, I was in a meeting at the White House about the Republican effort to rescind Obamacare (which ultimately died when McCain voted against it with his famous thumbs-down gesture). I told Trump that I was running for governor, and I was facing three opponents in the primary. I was willing to vote to defund Obamacare, but it was going to hurt me in my gubernatorial race. I told him I could use his support. He said that none of my opponents had ever done anything for him. "You were with me from the beginning," he said. "I'm going to support you. You'll be the next governor if it's up to me."

I appreciated his backing. Trump has a strong sense of loyalty, and he doesn't forget people who supported him. More important, though, I believed many of his policies were good for Ohio. He has continued to back me, and I still consider him a friend. I remember one trip on Air Force One, from Washington to Cincinnati, and the president came in, pointed at me, and told his senior advisors, "This is a guy who was with me from Day One, and he's never left me, and I'm never going to leave him."

🔴 🔴 🔴

John Kasich spent most of his career in politics, culminating in his run for Ohio governor in 2010. He studied politics, too, at Ohio State and went to work as a researcher for the Ohio Legislative Service Commission after graduating. He ran for office himself in 1978 and was elected to the state Senate when he was just twenty-six years old. He later won a seat in the U.S. House in 1982 and stayed there until 2001, by which time he had become part of the problem, like so many other long-timers in Congress. Even then, it was clear he had his eye on higher office, and he ran for president in 2000. After his defeat, he spent some time in the business world as an investment banker, but by 2009, he returned to politics and beat incumbent Democratic Governor Ted Strickland in a tight race. He easily won re-election in 2014, but by then it was clear that what he really wanted was another shot at the White House. Kasich's aspirations were typical of today's political environment. Even as he was asking voters to reelect him governor, he was preparing for his next move.

I felt that in his thirst for the presidency, Kasich increasingly ignored the issues facing Ohio. We ranked in the bottom third of all states in terms of job growth because of the declining manufacturing sector, yet we were probably in the top ten in terms of the tax burden on individual residents. People were leaving the state for better jobs and lower living costs elsewhere, and our politicians, starting with Governor Kasich, didn't seem to care. Even today, Ohio's tax revenue has not reached the level it was at prior to the 2008 recession. Of course, that hasn't stopped state officials from increasing spending. Just like their counterparts in Washington, no money seems to be no problem. They spend on, unworried about the consequences because they know they'll be out of office before the effects of runaway spending hit the pocketbooks of average Ohioans.

Rather than address these issues, Kasich traveled the country, essentially applying for a different job than the one voters had just hired him to do. He spent 177 days out of the state in 2016, taking his state-funded security detail with him. Travel costs soared to almost $476,000 from $17,000 — the state was spending more, on average, each month than it had spent for the entire year in 2014.

Kasich wasn't just out of touch with the issues facing most Ohioans, he was aloof. For one thing, he didn't like listening to what others had to say. He preferred to tell them what they should do. Although he didn't return phone calls, he did once agree to meet with me in person. Before I met then-candidate Trump at the IX Center, I went to meet Kasich at the governor's mansion, but he didn't show up. Something else came up, and he sent a staffer to meet me instead.

Kasich likes to portray himself as an economic hero for Ohio, but it wasn't his policies that turned the state around, it was President Trump's. Ohio's job growth numbers were dismal during Kasich's first seven years in office. It was only in his last year that the economy showed signs of significant improvement, which was a direct result of the federal tax cuts that the president championed. The tax breaks benefited manufacturers and encouraged hiring. Kasich's policies, when he even chose to focus on them, did nothing.

In the gubernatorial primary, I ran on my theme of strengthening the state financially. Needless to say, I didn't get Kasich's endorsement.

I patterned my approach after George Voinovich, who was governor from 1991 to 1998, and who froze spending after taking office. Then, he went to each of his department heads and asked them to cut 5 percent to 10 percent from their budgets.

I proposed a similar spending freeze that would last two years. I also called for stopping the expansion of Medicaid. Just as entitlement programs have swelled to almost three-fourths of the federal budget, state budgets are plagued by the same problems of fiscal bloat. Medicaid accounts for 42 percent of Ohio's budget, and it continues to grow. Expanding it meant spending more money we didn't have.

For me, the bottom line was clear: We had a Washington politician running the state, and he allowed Washington-like problems to fester. Kasich wasn't really interested in doing what he needed to do to fix our state because all he really wanted to do was run for president. I was determined to change that. I wanted to fix our state's finances and implement effective fiscal policy in a way I never could in Washington. I planned to inject some sanity into how the state handled its finances, especially how the money is distributed to the local level. For example, in his 2019 budget, the current governor, Mike DeWine, proposed an 18 percent increase in the gasoline tax. He was pushing it by saying that every county and every city will get more dollars sent to them by the state as a result of higher tax revenue. I met with local officials, who said they were glad for the extra money. I had several of these conversations, which all went much the same way, but I remember one in particular. The local trustee said they expected to see a revenue increase of about $340,000 from the new tax. I asked how many vehicles operated in their county, and they said about 15,000. I took out a piece of paper and did some math: If we assumed each of those 15,000 vehicles drive an average of 10,000 miles a year and get an average of twenty miles to the gallon, then the eighteen-cents-a-mile tax was going to generate about $1.35 million. So, if they went with their own tax increase, they were giving up more than a million dollars a year in taxes collected in their county. They hadn't thought it through.

The same thing happens at the federal level. People are short-sighted, and all they can see is the money that they're being offered, not the costs. We often forget that the less we have to give the government, the better off we are. Think about what happens at tax time. We pay the government a share of our paychecks every two weeks, but come tax time, we're excited about getting a refund. We even think the refund is like free money, but it's not. It's just what we lent to the government, interest-free, for the past year.

As the race heated up, two of my opponents combined their campaigns. That put me at a financial disadvantage, although I still believed I would prevail. Meanwhile, a Senate race was also underway. State Treasurer Josh Mandel was running against the incumbent Democrat, Sherrod Brown. Before the primary, though, Mandel announced he was dropping out of the race. That left the Republicans without a strong candidate in an important race against a key incumbent in a battleground state. There was less than a month until the filing deadline.

I flew to Washington and met with several senior White House officials, who encouraged me to switch races and run against Brown for the Senate. I didn't meet with the president himself that day — he had a scheduling conflict — but it was clear to me he wanted me in the race. Later, during a trip to Cincinnati, he publicly asked me to get into the race. I wasn't thrilled at the prospect of coming back to Washington. I'd been looking forward to dealing with issues that mattered to real people. I changed my mind because the president asked. As a senator, you do have more power. The rules of the Senate give each Senator far more independence, and with only a hundred Senators, each one has far more pull. What's more, I thought I might be in a better position to support the president and his agenda. If I was in the Senate, I might be able to help advance that agenda, and that would be good for Ohio and the country. On January 10, 2018, I made it official: I was running for the Senate.

🐾 🐾 🐾

Brown has been a senator since 2005, and he was well-known statewide. He was banking on that name recognition, as well as the huge $23 million war chest he'd amassed. Remember when I said that war chests can be a powerful weapon? Well, I probably should have been seen Brown's war chest as a deterrent. Brown pumped a lot of money into the race, much of it devoted to smearing me with false statements in television ads. He accused me of making money from nursing homes because of legislation I supported in Congress, not paying taxes, being a lobbyist for a foreign government, and of using a strip club owner's private jet for my campaign travel.

It was all nonsense, and it's not worth rehashing campaign claims, but I want to make sure that people know the truth. I didn't own any nursing homes when I served in Congress; I appealed my taxes and won. It was an overreach of state government. I'm also a CPA, so I know a thing or two about how taxes work. Those claims resulted from one year — 2000 — in which a change in the tax laws affected one of my businesses. You don't pay your taxes while they're on appeal. As for being a lobbyist, I never was one. I had a company at one point that was looking at doing consulting work that could have been viewed as lobbying under federal law. Out of an abundance of caution, my lawyer registered all the company officers as lobbyists. I didn't even know she'd done it until it came up in the campaign. We never pursued that line of business, the company never operated, and to the extent it existed at all, it was only on paper. It was defunct long before I got into politics. As for the "jet," it was a forty-year-old prop plane owned by a real estate investor whose holdings included a shopping center that had a strip club in it. He let me use the plane, and I paid the operating costs. The sixty-seven-year-old pilot donated his time. It was actually cheaper than driving all over the state.

But as you can see, the truth is often more complicated than the allegations. And what's worse, if I had spent time getting the truth out, I wouldn't be spending time pushing a positive, proactive agenda — the one that mattered. I campaigned hard. I shook 50,000 hands across the state. I ran on my record in Congress and tried to promote my message of fiscal responsibility statewide.

But Brown had money, and he had a megaphone. He could buy a lot of TV ads attacking me, and I couldn't counteract the message. In the end, Brown simply had more money behind him, he had statewide name recognition, which I had to build, and he had the full backing of his party.

I jumped into the race assuming that the Republican Party would get behind me just like the Democratic Party got behind him. Ohio was a battleground state, or so I thought. Brown was a golden boy of the opposition. People were already talking about him running for president. If I won, it would be a big victory for the Republicans and, perhaps more important, for President Trump. I was told I'd be able to raise $20 million or $25 million quickly, but that didn't happen.

Soon after the election was final, Senate Majority Leader Mitch McConnell revealed the GOP did not plan to focus on Ohio, Pennsylvania, Michigan, or Wisconsin — key states for President Trump's 2016 victory. Instead of directing resources toward me, they sent them to campaigns in Missouri, North Dakota, Montana, and West Virginia. They poured money into states with smaller populations and left me on my own in Ohio. I got almost no help from the party. By not supporting candidates in states that backed Trump, it raises the question: Is the Republican Senate leadership content to lose the presidency to pick up a few smaller states?

I'm proud of my showing. Brown spent almost $33.5 million to win. I spent only $4.8 million. In TV advertising alone, I was outspent thirty-to-one. But I lost by only 151,000 net votes out of 4.4 million cast. He was not able to help his party, which lost statewide, and I clearly left him with no money to run for president. Members of the political elite can be beat, but you need money. And even then, it doesn't happen often.

In hindsight, the odds of my success were not good — probably less than 25 percent. I would never have gotten into a business deal that had a less than 25 percent chance of success, but I took on the challenge of the Senate race because the president wanted me to, and I wanted to support him just as I always had, hopefully by coming back to Washington in the Senate.

After I lost the race, I didn't hear from anyone in the party. It's lonely when you lose. I get it. But it happens. George Voinovich, who held almost every public office during his forty-six-year career, got crushed by fourteen points when he first ran for the Senate in 1988, despite being a popular and well-known mayor of Cleveland. Two years later, he ran for governor and won. Our current governor, Mike DeWine, got beat handily by Sherrod Brown in 2006.

I will always be thankful and appreciative for the two calls I got on the night of the election. One from Ivanka Trump, thanking me for running and all I had done for the president, and the other from Senator Rob Portman, the other senator from Ohio. But everyone else in the party ignored what I had just done. I forced a senior senator to spend all of his money protecting his seat and he was not able to help his party (the Democrats) win any statewide seat. He was also left with no money to advance his dream of a presidential campaign. Since that night I have had so many rank-and-file Republicans thank me for taking up that fight. But the party establishment just moved on. Once you lose, and you no longer wield power, the political class dismisses you. I get it. It's the system. But it's a system that is failing our country.

I was disappointed, but at the same time, I had accomplished one of my goals: I was out of Washington. I no longer had to be a part of the pervasive stagnation and lack of leadership that had wasted a decade that began with such hope and promise.

EPILOGUE

PREVENTING THE NEXT LOST DECADE

I wrote this book to explain, for those outside of Washington, why failure in our government continues to endure. But I also wrote it in the hope that by understanding what's going wrong, we can find a way to fix it.

It's easy to go into Congress and spend. It's much harder to go in and do what's right. Ten years after the wave of reformers took control, we're still, at all levels of government, spending without any concern for the long-term implications or the next generation. We just crossed $22 trillion in debt and are heading toward $30 trillion. No one is talking about it. This year we are running ever-larger deficits while ignoring the underlying cause of the debt, especially entitlement programs. We're doing the same thing at the state and local levels — spending without the ability to pay and kicking the can down the road. We continue to shirk our fiscal responsibility, and as long as we do, the new decade will be just as lost as the last one.

But it's not too late. Congress can take steps to fix the problem, and if the current members can't get the job done, then it's up to voters to remind them who's in charge.

Here are some steps that I believe would go a long way toward ending dysfunction in Washington and getting us back on the path to prosperity.

REGULAR ORDER

This is quite simply the proper way of doing things. Instead of taking shortcuts for political gain, Congress needs to get back to following regular order for crafting legislation. Bills should be drafted in committee and debated among all committee members. Then they should be presented to the committee chair, and if there are enough votes, passed to the floor of the House for more debate. In other words, we need to return to the "Schoolhouse Rock!" version of government and get Bill back to his proper place on Capitol Hill once again.

Committee chairs should focus on running their committees, and they should require members to pass one meaningful piece of legislation each month — one that can be passed with bipartisan support. And speaking of committee chairs, they should be freely elected by the committee members, not chosen by House leadership. Hearings should return to their original purpose of being a fact-finding tool for members of Congress so that they can make more-informed decisions. They should be conducted with the intent of getting testimony from witnesses with perspective on all aspects of an issue. They should be used to reinforce the party line.

BALANCED BUDGET

I've spent a good portion of this book talking about the budget challenges we face. It's no wonder Congress doesn't want to deal with entitlements and other spending issues, but the longer we procrastinate on dealing with the tough choices ahead, the harder those choices become. We need to restore the budgeting process, so that Congress every year passes as budget. Then, we need an annual Fiscal State of the Union, addressed to both houses of Congress, so that members get a clear financial picture. We need to eliminate the gimmicks — no more continuing resolutions, "paid-fors," Rules Committee hijinks of waiving budget requirements, and no emergency expenditures unless they're absolutely justified. If a member wants to push a bill that breaks the budget, he or she should have to go to the floor of the House and explain publicly why their bill is worth whatever our grandchildren will have to pay the Chinese to cover the cost. Rolling ten-year projections for costs need to be extended to twenty so that every member gets an accurate cost picture of the legislation before they vote. (Pushing the cost impact into the twenty-first year is much harder to do than pushing into the eleventh.)

Congress also must learn to say no. At least until the debt and deficit are under control, we must recognize that we have to make hard choices. Those won't always be popular, but they may be necessary. Taming the deficit should be a shared goal of both political parties, and they should agree to work together to achieve it — even if they can't agree on anything else.

To reinforce the importance of following a budget, every member of the House should be required to take a turn on the Budget Committee. That's where you learn what's really going on, but because no one wants to take the hard votes, the Budget Committee is Washington's equivalent of Siberia. Everyone who winds up there wants to get out as quickly as possible. If we made a rotation on Budget mandatory, it would force everyone to understand the hard choices we face.

TERM LIMITS

Incumbents' ability to raise money essentially allows them to stay in office as long as they want. Putting a limit on their length of service is the only answer. I believe our Founding Fathers actually envisioned limited terms; they just didn't think they had to spell it out. Remember, George Washington voluntarily left office after two terms, and that was the tradition for all presidents until Franklin Roosevelt stayed for a third amid World War II. Our founders assumed people would work and accomplish something in life, then serve in government out of a sense of civic duty and, ultimately, return to private life. They didn't foresee politics becoming a career, let alone a financial reward.

In addition, any limits need to be pure term limits. Some states, like Ohio, set limits on a specific office, but a candidate can jump back and forth between the House and the Senate for years. This undermines the spirit of term limits. What's needed at the federal level is strict limits on House and Senate seats. I would argue for a limit of five terms in the House and two in the Senate. And no person should be able to hold federal office for more than 16 years anywhere, including the presidency and vice presidency.

REFORM LEADERSHIP

Leadership positions in Congress have become too powerful. They have become a reward that members seek, often to the exclusion of all else. Committee chairs and the speaker need to be overseers and administrators, ensuring that members are following the proper protocol and that legislation is progressing as it should. They shouldn't be impeding the process or creating shortcuts that allow for partisan victories at the expense of sound policy.

In the House, the speaker position in particular needs to be returned to its original purpose of working for all members, not just one party. To that end, the House should consider electing a speaker who is not a member of Congress — an esteemed public servant who has proven their statesmanship but who no longer is beholden to political parties. In effect, lawmakers would hire an outside administrator, agreed upon by a majority from both parties. This would reduce the political gamesmanship, encourage better legislation and allow for more thorough and robust debate.

RESTRICT CAMPAIGN DONATIONS

We need to limit the amount of money coming into campaigns — but only after term limits are put in place. Otherwise, the longer candidates are in office, the harder they will become to defeat. Simply capping donations at the current limits of $2,700 per federal candidate for individuals and $5,000 a year for political action committees doesn't work. It's too easy to disguise or spread the money around. We need to limit donations by source, including the political parties. If we set a maximum amount each source can give to all candidates, we would squeeze a lot of money out of politics and destabilize the political machines.

VOTE FROM HOME

The main reason lawmakers go to Washington is to vote. If members could vote from home, we could save millions of dollars a year in travel costs and make government more efficient in the process. Think of the expense of flying all those members to D.C. every week. When I was in office, it cost me about $800 a week to go back and forth. Some districts are more remote, and it costs a lot more. Assume it's an average of $1,500 for all members of Congress — House and Senate. That's about $8 million a year. You could save a lot of that money by allowing members to vote from home.

As it stands right now, the only way to track your vote is for you to vote on the floor of the House, which means you have to be in Washington. But this is really just a matter of changing the rules of the House and Senate and setting up a secure website, with identity verification, to collect the votes.

CONCENTRATE COMMITTEE WORK

If lawmakers didn't have committee work and votes to cast, they would have nothing to do in Washington other than take meetings. All the associations and lobbying groups want to come by for a meeting, but to the extent that needs to be done at all, it doesn't have to be done in Washington. Make the lobbyists fan out across the country. Maybe the additional cost and inconvenience of having to visit each lawmaker in their home district will be a deterrent.

Rather than allowing committees to meet whenever they want, we should squeeze all the committee work into a few weeks and require that lawmakers stay in Washington until their work is done. Combined with voting from home, this would reduce unnecessary travel expense and force members to be more productive. Many state Legislatures already do this. In Texas, which is the second most populous state, lawmakers meet for only five months once every two years. It forces them to get things done. The longer the session, the more mistakes people can make.

Members will resist this change because they have to run home and raise money so frequently, but with the proper limits on campaign donations, they could shift their focus toward actually doing their jobs.

KNOW YOUR ADVERSARY

Washington has descended into tribalism and identity politics — "us" versus "them." Our government was founded on the notion of compromise. No matter how bitterly we disagree, everyone working to govern the country must recognize the need to cooperate. Yet today in Washington, compromise is a dirty word. Committee meetings are segregated by party. Democrats and Republicans have little interaction.

Committee chairs — elected by the members — can address this problem by requiring that the entire committee meet in the same room. Individual members can do what John Carney and I did: meet with each other. Sit down to breakfast. Share a bagel. Talk sports. Do whatever it takes to find common ground. If you're a Republican, go to the Democratic Club and vice versa. The opposing party isn't the enemy. We are all on the same side — the side of America and democracy. Disagreeing on policy is healthy. Refusing to speak to one another because we disagree isn't.

These are just a few ideas for how to make the federal government work better and get the legislative process back on track, so it's actually fixing problems that matter to people rather than helping the political elite score points and get ahead.

Since my term in Congress expired in January 2019, I have been traveling around Ohio speaking to different groups about these issues. Because I was unable to change the way the government operates from within, I have decided to try to change it from the outside.

Ohio, in particular, has the opportunity to benefit from President Trump's tax cuts and the regulatory changes that he's pushed through. Along with states like Pennsylvania, Michigan and Wisconsin, Ohio is benefiting from the Trump economy, and as long as that continues, I believe these states will support Trump in the next election.

I have doubts that the government will get its financial house in order, and I believe, as I said when I ran for governor, that states need to prepare themselves. To that end, I've formed the Ohio's Future Foundation, which looks at ways to encourage economic development around the state. We're forming a network of people who want to make their voices heard and change the way government operates.

It's a positive approach to what has proven so far to be an intractable problem. Despite my disillusionment with what I saw in Washington, I'm not bitter. While I believe our government has lost its way, I still believe in this great nation. Only in America could a poor kid from a steel mill town become a successful businessman, be elected to Congress and spend time with the president. By taking my message directly to the people, I hope that voters will become more focused on the issues, and elect more representatives not based on their popularity or personalities, but who will go to Washington to work for them.

In doing so, I hope to apply the lessons I learned living through the GOP's Lost Decade. If we are successful, we may be able to keep the malaise from spreading into the next ten years.

ACKNOWLEDGMENTS

Going to Washington and serving in Congress was never something I planned, and it was an honor to be there serving my state and my country.

One thing I learned from my experience was that although our system is broken, it is still unmatched by any other country in the world. It is a governmental system that allows hard work and effort to be rewarded with the ability to live the American Dream. My parents taught me that early and the state of Ohio gave me that opportunity.

I want to thank all those who serve our great nation whether at the federal, state, or local level, as well as the military men and woman who protect our ability to have a free nation. Although not perfect, it is the best in the world.

I want to thank Noam Neusner, Loren Steffy, and the entire 30 Point team who worked with me every step of the way on this book from inception to completion.

To my family, I will be forever indebted, especially my parents, whose unwavering love and support taught me that anything is possible in life with hard work and dedication.

Most of all, I want to thank my wife, Tina, who has been at my side every step of the way through this wonderful journey called life.

Although this book captures only one decade, it was an important decade in my life. It was a decade that gave me an opportunity to serve my country — a country that afforded me an opportunity to live the American Dream.

INDEX

A

B

T

U

V

W